Much Ado About COACHING

Much Ado About
COACHING

EDITED BY

Charlotte Rydlund
Nicholas Wai
Yvonne Thackray

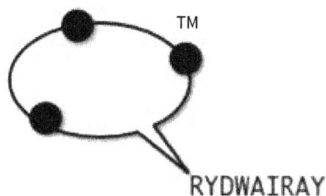

TM

RYDWAIRAY

Most of the material in this book first appeared on the World Wide Web in 2012-2014 on www.the-goodcoach.com

First Printing: 2014

ISBN 978-0-9938333-0-4

RYDWAIRAY: Hong Kong | London | Halifax

www.muchadoaboutcoaching.com

Special discounts are available on quantity purchases by corporations, associations, educators, and others. For details, contact the publisher at: info@muchadoaboutcoaching.com

Contents

Preface

What is coaching? That's a great question! Why? Because if we were to ask a hundred people what coaching means to them, we would probably get a hundred different answers which would overlap, but not necessarily coincide. Although coaching has been around for almost five decades, it has only recently been formalised and professionalised as a discipline. We are three coaches from different parts of the world who met by chance and decided to work together and explore executive coaching, based on our different experiences and locations. As participants in the field, we wanted to make people familiar with what coaching is, and raise awareness of how it can contribute to personal and professional well-being.

This book explores many different aspects of coaching. Our aim is not just to provide a perspective on what coaching is and can be, but also to provide key insights from our experiences as professional coaches.

Who are we writing for? This book is for everyone curious about coaching!

- Professionals who have been or will be clients
- Leaders who have already had coaching, and are applying techniques in their roles
- Coaches who have just completed their training and are starting out
- Coaches who are seeking alternative perspectives for continuing their professional development

Being curious and actively following through is a cornerstone for learning and growth, and is vital for coaching. It opens up new possibilities and sparks new conversations – and that is also our aim in this book.

Change and transition are key themes in *Much Ado About Coaching*. In this book, experienced coaches from all over the world share their perspectives on change, growth, and evolution, with reference to both their professional and personal experiences. Particularly inspirational was the experience of author and editor Charlotte Rydlund, who underwent a profound change in her life when she left her role as a multinational corporate executive and internal coach to follow her passion as an entrepreneur. Her transition began with an advocacy project: a four-month diving expedition whose aim was to mobilize communities to clean up the underwater environment across Canada and raise awareness through online and offline media. When the expedition ended, Charlotte actualized her transition and now works as a certified change management coach and entrepreneur who empowers leaders and business owners to grow and succeed. leaders and business owners to grow and succeed. This experience inspired her to write a series of essays on what she learned about herself on her journey.

We hope you will share all of our ups and downs, our triumphs and setbacks, as well as our insights and epiphanies. This book in your hand (or on your screen) is the labour of love, not just for the three of us, but also for the many friends and collaborators who helped make it possible. We hope this book inspires your transition as much as it inspired us!

CHAPTER 1

WHAT IS COACHING?

The social landscape of coaching: an overview

Yvonne Thackray

The practice and language of coaching emerged as a 'new derivative of the best thinking in self-improvement... and most recently in the business world, where it exploded into the corporate environment in the 1990s'.[1] Coaching is an amalgamation of multiple theories and practices from a broad array of disciplines, all of which share a common goal: 'unlocking a person's potential to maximise their own performance'.[2] They include:

- **The social sciences.** Psychology has significantly influenced the field of coaching thus far; and management and leadership, human resources, linguistics, sociology, philosophy and anthropology are increasingly making contributions to the field of coaching through their theories on human social behaviour, relationships and communication.

- **Adult education, learning, and development.** The process of continual personal and professional development requires a very different approach to that used to educate young adults. It is about creating a space for motivated adults, who choose to bring their accumulated knowledge and work experiences and combine them with educational knowledge to enhance their learning and development and achieve their goals.

1 Williams, P. (20 Jan 2004). Coaching and Mentoring International Seminar.
2 Whitmore, J. (1992). *Coaching for Performance*.

- **Eastern, Western, and other philosophies.** Philosophy is primarily used as a guiding principle for behaviour, and it is often based on the fundamental idea of asking questions to gain understanding and insights about the nature of knowledge, existence and reality. Philosophical concepts can be integrated into coaching, and philosophy has particularly influenced evidence-based coaching, but it is not necessarily incorporated into core coaching practices.

- **The performing arts.** Coaching can utilise the techniques actors use to embody emotions, create memories and portray characters. These skills can help clients develop their inner awareness and presence.

- **Systems theory.** Adapting concepts of feedback and feed-forward loops provides a meta-approach for dealing with chaos.[3]

With many possible approaches at their disposal, coaches tend to specialize in a number of pathway(s) to work with clients on challenges which might include leadership, personal well-being, performance, presence, work-life balance, supporting transitions during a promotion (on boarding), and so on. The coach's expertise and ability to create a safe space allows the client to reflect (verbally, emotionally, and through their body language) and proactively find new ways to deal with the challenges we face in an increasingly fast-paced and complex society. Coaching enables clients to reach their goals, and whatever goal is important to a client, the coach's motto should be 'it's not just about being a good coach, it's being good at being a good coach'.[4]

---

3 Brock, V. (2008). 'Grounded Theory of the Roots and Emergence of Coaching'.

4 Paraphrased from Herzfeld, *The Poetics of Manhood* (1985).

The humanist school of psychology as the predecessor to coaching

Nicholas Wai

Creating the right environment, setting the appropriate context, and being present are all vital for achieving success in many activities. In the world of coaching, 'active listening' and the cultivation of an 'empathetic relationship' which is 'client-focused' is considered standard practice. This may seem like common sense as trained coaches when we coach our clients to resolve their issues or make changes. However in the 1950s therapists and psychiatrists commonly believed that they possessed all the answers and should set the agenda, and treated their clients as objects rather than people. It was Carl Rogers who changed all that.

Carl Rogers belonged to the humanist school of psychology, which emerged at a time when many psychologists had become frustrated with the psychoanalytic school (which focused mostly on the past) and the behavioural school (which was mechanistic in its assumptions about human behaviour). Humanist therapists, by contrast, focussed on finding the best in people and exploring their potential to grow and self-actualise. To achieve this aim, the humanists believed that therapists had to build a strong relationship and active partnership with their clients by being present and fully engaged in the healing process, thus enabling their clients to trust themselves enough to draw on their own resources to resolve their issues. This way of thinking was novel at the time, but proved decidedly useful for highly functional and mentally healthy people – a group which was not much studied by psychologists at the time, though they certainly were well represented in the population at large. Rogers and the humanist school provided a useful approach to help these people develop their full potential. Hence, it is not surprising that coaching emerged and developed to cater to this section of the population in an era in which more people than ever performed mental rather than physical work.

How then does 'being present and fully engaged' occur in a coaching relationship? It helps the coach to be empathic, to be able to focus fully on the client without interference from his/her own judgement or evaluation, to listen to what's being said and not said, to be more aware of the body language and emotions displayed, and to ask the right questions in a way that is both challenging and respectful. This in turn enables the client to focus on the 'now', thus enabling creativity and possibilities to flow freely, without hindrance from the past or future. The discipline of being present and fully engaged as a coach and creating a safe and confidential space in which the client can empower himself or herself is the purpose of coaching, and it is the next logical step from humanist therapy.

Being sensitive: a cultural perspective on action and choice

Charlotte Rydlund

A**ction** is defined by the *Oxford English Dictionary* as: 'the fact or process of doing something, typically to achieve an aim'. This means that to perform an action, you are required to be doing something. When you do something, it means that in some way you have made a choice to do it. Whether it's a conscious or unconscious choice, whether it's under your own or someone else's directive, action means that a choice was made. By being courageous and taking responsibility for the choices you make, your actions are more likely to be in line with your own intended outcomes rather than dictated by social or cultural expectations.

Choices can be pro-active or forced, passive or socially mandated, and can be influenced by environmental, financial, health, or career factors – I could go on. But of course this assumes that you have a choice, or that you believe you have a choice. Having a choice means being able to choose from more than one option. I often hear the phrase, 'I didn't have a choice'. Is that really true? What internal (psychological state, past experiences) or external factors (social, cultural, business, personal, financial) might be influencing you? What might it take to transform a person 'without choices' into a person with choices? I'm naturally a positive person, so I believe there is always a choice. That being said, sometimes it takes some self-awareness, willpower, and a healthy dose of non-judgmental curiosity to make that mental transition.

So how do choices and action become influenced by culture? I believe culture influences choices (and therefore actions) in a big way. In some cultures the social expectation is to marry within your own religion, or society might expect you to get a university degree or to follow a certain career path. I imagine there may even be social or cultural perceptions regarding skydiving or playing drums. These types of social and cultural factors influence choice and therefore action. Do you keep to the social or cultural expectations? Do you rebel against them? Either way it's a choice, and the action will follow.

I often hear the phrase 'that's how I've always done it'. What does that mean in this context? Doing what you've always done means you are choosing to pursue the same course you've always taken. So this is a choice, and the action (and most likely result) that follow are based on that choice. Doing what you've always done can simply be a path of least resistance, or it could be culturally or socially directed. Whatever the reason, it is important to understand that doing the same thing will result in the same outcome. This reminds me of a quote from Albert Einstein: 'Insanity: doing the same thing over and over again and expecting different results'. But what if we want a different outcome?

If we want a different outcome, then we need to choose a different action. Meaning that we most likely can't choose the path of least resistance (doing what we've always done before). So, wanting a different outcome must somehow require different input. This implies that somewhere along the way, a choice must be made to do something differently. This could be doing something you have never done before, rebelling against a social or cultural expectation, or following your dream instead of a prescribed career path. Choosing and then doing something different from what you've done before increases the chances that you will get a different result. Maybe even a result that is closer to your personal intended outcome.

Performance = potential - interference, enhanced by honesty, bravery and responsibility

Nicholas Wai

I **recently** had the good fortune to be able to sit in on a fascinating leadership workshop by a fellow coach and friend, C. Originally from Hong Kong, C has been a pioneer in coaching and training in China, with students coming from almost all the major cities. This particular workshop was organised by the continuing education department of a university for senior managers in Chinese corporations in Shenzhen, just north of Hong Kong.

I have been to similar workshops before, but never have I witnessed such effective explanations and demonstrations of theoretical concepts, which most participants were able to immediately understand and utilise to bring about transformational personal growth. Yes, it was that amazing! C takes her responsibility, and her students' responsibility for learning and growth, very seriously. Holding honesty to be of the utmost importance both for herself and for her students, she would not move on to another topic until her point had been fully taken in and learning had taken place. I admire that in her, and reflected on several occasions when I had skirted around an issue to avoid awkwardness, thus potentially robbing my client of an opportunity for growth and learning. The key to her approach was her insistence on getting permission from her students.

One of the concepts that was discussed in the workshop came from Timothy Gallway's *The Inner Games of Tennis.* He proposed that performance (p) is equal to potential (P) minus interference (I), or p=P-I. Without interference, performance would equal potential, but as we all know that's not always the case. What stops us could be a lack of necessary skills, drive, motivation, or confidence in ourselves, but fear, overconfidence or a lack of grounding in the present could also be factors.

During reflective moments, my fellow students and I would discover that we often obstruct our own progress with self-limiting or even self-sabotaging behaviours. To remove these obstructions and move forward, it helps to find our own unique way(s) to be more grounded and build compassion for ourselves and others (for example, meditation). Thus we can be comfortable in our own skins and more able to appreciate and empathise with others, and be more grateful for all the good things in our life so we can replace our negative self-communications with positive ones.

Identifying psychological obstructions in a particular situation will not only help us to better understand our behaviours, it also allows us to recognise the subconscious thoughts that drive them. It also allows us to take responsibility in making conscious choices to drive desired behaviours. In order to confront the truth and not skirt around short-term awkwardness, we need to be brave and honest with ourselves and be willing to take responsibility for our actions. With willpower and constant practice we can realise our potential with ease and grace.

Is coaching really a profession?

Yvonne Thackray

I**s coaching** really a profession? What a strange question to ask – after all, I consciously added 'professional' in my career title. The subtle difference is in the language – professional and profession. Being professional embodies a set of qualities including formal and/or vocation education, working experience, and continuing professional and personal development, which are often observed and assessed (positively/negatively) during interactions with the client. It is about an individual's attitude towards their role, job or career. A profession, on the other hand, involves a collective body in which all of its members agree to abide by a code, and allow their professional practice to be critically evaluated by their peers. For a vocation to qualify as a profession and achieve a status equal to that of some other professional careers e.g. lawyers, accountants, engineers, doctors etc. it needs to include:

- Significant barriers to entry
- A shared common body of knowledge rather than proprietary systems
- Formal qualifications at tertiary level
- Regulatory bodies with the power to admit, discipline and meaningfully sanction members
- An enforceable code of ethics
- Some form of state-sanctioned licensing or regulation[5]

---

5 Grant, A & Cavanagh, M (2004). 'Towards a Profession of coaching: Sixty-Five Years of Progress for the Future'.

The coaching industry is working on all fronts to move towards being accepted as a profession. For example, there is a growing amount of evidence-based research being performed and reported, giving quantifiable evidence of the impact of coaching for different niches from the perspectives of both client and coach, and the effectiveness of different coaching approaches. In addition, the ICF and EMCC have jointly filed with the European Union a code of ethics as a benchmark for the profession.

There are many representatives in the coaching field. Each representative has a focussed mission based on specific themes important to their members, and some representatives are working together towards building a common body of knowledge for coaches and the market i.e. buyers of coaching services. For example, the Association for Professional Executive Coaching and Supervision (APECS) and the Graduate School Alliance of Executive Coaching (GSEAC) both focus solely on executive coaching; the International Coach Federation (ICF), the International Association of Coaching (IAC), European Mentoring and Coaching Council (EMCC), and the Association for Coaching (AC) look at both life coaching and executive coaching. Other representatives have established themselves based on location. Examples include the Czech Association of Coaches (CAKO), the Société Francaise de Coaching (SFC), Der Deutsche Bundesverband Coaching e.V. (DBVC), Asia Pacific Alliance of Coaches (APAC), and the Associação Brasileira de Coaching Executivo e Empresarial (ABRACEM), to just name a few. Universities are also offering tertiary-level courses in coaching in Australia, UK, South Korea, France, and the USA.

The industry is still in of its infancy, and it will take considerable time for coaching to attain professional status. Anybody who provides professional coaching should be aware of what's happening in the industry, and support the evolution of coaching. However, the road towards become a profession will not be an easy one, as many challenges lie ahead.

Reframing obstacles with self-coaching: a personal reflection

Charlotte Rydlund

Almost every day there is at least one thing that I get annoyed about. It can be something like being stuck in traffic, losing battery power on my smartphone, a slow internet connection, or not finding a key ingredient for a recipe (like bamboo shoots) in the local store. Ring a bell?

These are small things (or an accumulation of things) that end up making a day seem stressful, possibly because when things come up that are different from what I was planning, I feel like I might lose focus from achieving my goals. I describe these occurrences as annoyances or obstacles that often pop up and take up time and energy from my day. Over time, I have worked on becoming more self-aware of when such occurrences trigger an 'annoyed' reaction in me. It usually starts with my stomach tightening. There are three stories I use when I am faced with daily obstacles, they are my strategies to reframe situations that could otherwise divert my focus.

1. In the book *The Tao of Pooh* by Benjamin Hoff, life is described as a river. The flow of the river is life, and rocks of different shapes and sizes that come up in the river are the obstacles that occur along the way. When these rocks show up in the river (the flow of life), you can choose what happens to that flow: i) you can let that rock stop your flow, and pressure (stress) builds up as the flow pushes you against the obstacle;. ii) you can flow around that rock; iii) you can flow over the rock; or iv) sometimes the rock will move all by itself.

When thinking about this story, I remind myself that I can choose how I respond to annoyances which arise. Do I choose to let it stop or bother me? Do I find an alternate route around the rock? Will the rock move? More often than not, I find that my mindset changes when I think of this story, and whatever the rock may be, it suddenly feels less annoying or stressful than it did before. In essence, you can choose how you respond to obstacles, and with that choice, you can replace negative emotions like annoyance or stress with positive/productive ones.

2. There is a Swedish comedy show called *Hipp Hipp*. Although it is in the southern Swedish accent (Skånska), which is usually more difficult to follow for foreign-speakers, I can follow most of it, and it is a great show. There is one skit called 'dagens i-lands problem', which translates to 'today's First World problem'. In these skits, you might see someone swearing at post-it notes that won't stick to their computer monitor, or someone cursing at the TV while trying to find the right remote amongst umpteen different ones on the table. The punchline is always 'today's First World problem'.

I think of this when I'm faced with annoyances, such as this example: I love cooking, and one time, I had planned on making a Thai curry. Bamboo shoots are vital for the recipe, so when I discovered the local store didn't have any, I felt my stomach slowly tightening, and thoughts like, 'I can't find bamboo shoots at the local store? How is this possible? This is a key ingredient in making Thai curry!' went through my mind. This was when I took a deep breath and said to myself, 'today's First World problem'. Because, in the end, that's all it is. I can live without bamboo shoots, or go somewhere else to find them. It's not a big deal and not a matter of life or death. There are so many other problems in the world that are worth focusing my energy on than a lack of bamboo shoots.

3. I saw a Canadian comedy show live in London, England several years ago. I don't remember what it was called, but it was very funny and very Canadian. One of the skits involved an exaggerated home-shopping TV show host who could solve all your problems with three simple words. The hilarious banter between the host and actors embedded amongst the audience was that his jingle was made up of four words combined to make three. To keep things polite, I will not repeat the whole jingle here, but the essence of it was '****ing get over it'.

This is another story I think of when I get annoyed. Sometimes I just need to '****ing get over it'. Usually by the time I think of this third story, I've already gotten over it, but it helps to get over whatever the issue is once and for all.

To summarize the essence of the stories that I use to reframe annoyances in life:

- I can choose how I deal with the rocks (obstacles/ annoyances) that arise in life

- Today's First World problem?

- '****ing get over it'

What strategies do you use?

CHAPTER 2

MAKING CHANGES: BY CHOICE OR CIRCUMSTANCE

Kilometer 0: the decision

Charlotte Rydlund

Change is the only thing that is constant. However, change comes in many forms. This is the first of a six-part series to document my career transition from seven years in the corporate world to working independently as an executive coach. In terms of scale, this change was a big one and it was a change I chose to make.

Why did I choose this new path? It took time for me to get to this point, slowly turning unconscious or subconscious actions into conscious ones. Even though coaching was not my full-time job, I had been coaching managers at different levels and in different corporate and organizational environments for almost 10 years. Over the last two years, it became increasingly clear to me that my passion was coaching people to help them succeed, and I wanted to pursue it full time. At that time I did not know how I was going to transform this passion into my new career path, nor did I feel the need to jump into it right then, but I began making choices that would take me in the right direction.

These choices included getting certified in executive coaching at Columbia University, increasing the amount of coaching I did internally at work, and then finally leaving my full-time position as a Marketing Manager at Procter & Gamble. However, other choices we made as a family – to leave Switzerland and set up an independent business in Canada. So, not only was I doing a complete switch in career path, but I was also relocating to a new region that I had yet to discover.

This gives you a little background on what this series is about. I will document my transition, and share my experiences and tips that I found helpful along the way. I was excited, a little scared, but absolutely confident and committed to this change. I could not have gotten where I am without support of family, friends, and some meaningful coaching sessions too. Yes, even coaches seek out coaching!

Leaving my job after almost seven years of strategic sourcing and marketing in a corporate environment was initially quite a shock to the system. Monday mornings were the strangest. I would wake up thinking I needed to go to work, and then realize that I didn't. I couldn't relax or sit still for the first three weeks. Our apartment became *very* clean and organized as I kept myself busy. I suppose I was trying to replace the constant stimulation of a working environment at home. Although I was being told, 'you need to relax, take some time to unwind', I was not in the mindset to listen to or appreciate that kind of good advice!

A few tips after making a big decision:

- **Take time for yourself to readjust.** This was probably the best advice I was given by family and friends – to take that time for myself, but not directly after leaving the company. And it was true; I needed that first month to readjust in order to be mentally open for what was to come. I chose to attend a four-day yoga retreat about a month after leaving the corporate world, and this is when my 'new' world began to re-centre around a routine that no longer included the traditional activity of 'going to work'.

- **Create a new routine.** This was the second most helpful aspect in my first weeks and months of transitioning out of a Monday-to-Friday, 9-to-5 (or 7!) job. For me this included getting up the same time every day, setting certain tasks with clear priorities to do each day and week that would contribute towards setting up the business, spending quality time with family, and keeping to a daily exercise regimen. Having a schedule helped me to stay focused on the new path I had chosen.

- **Stay in touch with your network.** I have often found that when people leave a job, change assignments, or move country, you can quickly lose touch with them. I enjoy being with people, and learn something new from every conversation and interaction. It was (and is) important to me to stay in touch with people I had built strong working relationships with, so I made that a priority. It takes effort, but that effort is well worth it. Staying in touch with my network, with friends and family, has been an essential part of my transition.

- **Be present in the moment.** There are many ways to be distracted, especially when readjusting to a new life and routine. It can feel like chaos, with so many different balls up in the air at once, and you need to find a way to juggle them all. I found it extremely helpful to focus on one thing at a time, and to truly be present while doing it: be it coaching, reading, meeting people, planning an international move, working on a business plan, cooking dinner or walking by the lake with our Labrador. Although I focused on being in the moment and enjoying the present, I kept very busy and did not take the time to reflect (until now).

- **Take time to reflect.** Days and weeks go by fast. It feels like only yesterday that I was still going to work, and in a blink, six months had already gone past. Writing this series was my own way of reflecting on my transition and sharing a few things I learned along the way.

Cultural pressures – submit or transcend?

Nicholas Wai

Being forced to take some time off when I was sick gave me the chance to re-watch a Japanese movie called *Railways* – a moving story about a financially successful 'salaryman' who realised his childhood dream of becoming an electric train driver at 49. I'm not a train buff particularly (aircraft are more my thing), but the story of life transformation grabbed my attention while on a flight a few years ago. In Japanese society (as in western cultures), social expectations often dictate what jobs one should hold, how much one should earn, where one should live, and what one should wear or drive. These status symbols, observable 'badges of honour' inform others, and ourselves, of our identity, worth, and status. You may recognise some of these 'badges' in your society. In the movie, the main character is a senior executive within a power company who lives in the city with his wife and daughter, and they are all busy leading their separate lives. He doesn't particularly like his job, but it pays well. For a long time he hadn't thought about what he really wanted to do, until his mother suddenly fell ill in the countryside and a dear friend who always used to ask if he is 'living well' passed away.

These two sudden and unexpected 'surges' force him to finally reflect on what is truly important for him. He quits his job, moves back to the countryside to be closer to his mother, and applies for the job he had dreamed of in his childhood. The social stigma resulting from what could be considered a demotion (or career suicide!) didn't matter to him, as he was totally committed to his new dream job. It gave him a purpose and an opportunity to rebuild his relationship with his daughter, who also followed him to the countryside – and also gave him the opportunity to truly live his life.

These heart-warming stories are often dismissed as unrealistic, but if we suspend our judgement for a moment and just spend some time delving into the film's message, which person do we admire more – the senior executive in the city, or the train driver in the countryside?

Each of us will have our own opinion, based on our own values and circumstances. The common measures of success in modern society focus on status and money rather than happiness and family relationships, and many of us will be persuaded to pick the former career (senior executive) than the latter (train driver). However, according to a hospital nurse who cares for dying patients, the most common regrets of people on their deathbeds[6] is that they wish they had not lived according to the expectations of others, had worked less, and had spent more time on things that made them happier and closer to their families.

Societal norms are powerful, and it's not always easy to act against them. I believe that the key thing is to truly understand what's important to us and what makes us tick. With these as our compass, we will be more able to make conscious choices about what is best for us, and not blame culture or society for how we live our lives. We may not be able to immediately transcend our cultural or societal norms, but what we can do is to focus on doing more of the things we enjoy doing whilst reducing the impact of things that go against our values. It's a fine balance we can all learn to handle.

---

6 [website] *Top five regrets of the dying | Life and style | the guardian*

Changing families, changing roles

Yvonne Thackray

Just as our personal circumstances are always changing, our familial support networks are also evolving. I recently read a particularly interesting feature in *The Economist* entitled 'Changing families: The Post Nuclear Age'[7] (March 16th 2013) that documents how society in the UK is changing. The 'traditional' family, which is a remnant of the Victorian era of a 'two parent, male-breadwinner family', is something of the past. The professional and educational status of the family's eldest adult male no longer dictates where a family belongs within the UK's social structure. An interesting fact: the number of marriages has collapsed to Victorian levels since the 1980s whilst the number of divorces annually has increased from 16,000 in 1945 to over 117,000 to date.

A number of factors have led to a revaluation and reinterpretation of the family and the roles within it. This includes the emancipation of women (which began during the nineteenth and early twentieth centuries), and changes in national social and economic policies, which focussed on consumerism and a reduction in social welfare available to its citizens. Both parents are generally required to work to maintain an acceptable standard of living. The article identifies three broadly defined family types: the university-educated professional classes, the working classes, and the immigrants. The educated professional classes (white collar) typically hold onto old-fashioned ideals of marriage whereby the husband is primarily earner and provide for his family, and married professional women generally wait until they are in their early 30s before having their first child as they put

7 [website] *Changing families: The post-nuclear age | The Economist*

their careers first. The working classes are those who do 'routine' or 'semi-routine' (blue collar) manual jobs. More children in this class are being born out of wedlock. Overall though women are less dependent on the spouse's income because of either the UK's generous welfare system and/or women's capability to out earn their partner's income (according to reports from the Resolution Foundation). The final group, immigrants who came to the UK in search of better opportunities, are described as being more conservative, though the article does not describe or define what this means – but over several generations they generally adapt to British norms.

What this article highlights is the increasingly complex society that each individual has to engage with: they have to balance social expectations and individual desires which influences how they prioritize their needs, and must decide what approaches are available to them to deal with their situation. It also hints about the shifts in expectations about marriage. Nowadays marriage is expected to be about finding a partner for emotional well-being whereas in previous decades couples would often marry in their early 20s as a practical step towards building a family. The societal landscape is changing, and it is creating a state of uncertainty that leads us to question our place and role in society – as an individual, partner, citizen, parent, child and professional worker – and this can lead to success in some areas and confusion in others. Being aware of these changes and asking probing questions about what we take for granted, reflecting on them and finding our truths will help us to regain balance and a sense of calmness in the complex and stressful lives we now live in 'the new normal'.

Exit statements: choosing a positive attitude in the midst of career transition

Naomi Dishington

Choosing to leave a job can be a liberating experience (as Charlotte Rydlund's articles on her career transition show) – but the shock of being fired (or 'out-placed') is quite a different experience. I recently had the opportunity to participate in a two-day career transition workshop for out-placed professionals as a supporting facilitator, and this provided me with some further interesting perspectives on managing unexpected career transitions. One of the first steps in the course was to help participants become aware of their emotions regarding their recent job loss, and to begin to manage these emotions. Some people experienced anger; some feared being unable to provide for their families; others were actually relieved to be out of dead-end jobs and eager to explore more challenging roles. Despite a wide variety of life circumstances, every person in the room faced challenges to his/her identity because of their unexpected job loss.

After group members shared their thoughts and emotions, our next step was to guide them through the very important task of crafting a positive 'exit statement'. An exit statement is designed to answer the inevitable (and dreaded) question: 'So, why are you looking for a job?' The way in which one answers that question will convey a powerful message, both to oneself and to the listener. Writing an exit statement provides an opportunity to carefully choose the words, story, and focus you will embrace during your job transition. Choosing a resilient, positive attitude is key; it will manifest as the persona you share with the world.

Probably the most challenging and also the most vital part of the exit statement exercise was learning to describe the out-placing experience without anger, negativity or placing blame. Since the statements needed to be short, simple, and non-defensive, it required the speakers to shift from defeatist or negative attitudes, such as, 'I was unfairly let go,' or 'My boss hated me,' to optimistic mentalities, like: 'My job was eliminated due to restructuring, but I've learned a lot and am eager to leverage my experience toward a challenging new role.' Clearly the second sentence reflects a much more marketable and attractive attitude for a potential new hire. It also lifts the spirits of the speaker, thus helping him to articulate a positive new plan for the future.

The task of creating concise exit statements was difficult, but had profound results. Creating positive statements impacts our attitude about ourselves, our outlook for the future, and possibly even our chances of landing a new job, because the way in which we name and share our experience will potentially open or close doors of opportunity. The exit statement becomes a personal mantra that we play like a loop tape in our minds. We must be deliberate in creating strong, positive, forward-looking statements in order to effectively motivate and market ourselves.

As I coached several group members through the creation of their exit statements, I was struck by how powerfully this exercise impacted their emotional states. Some who had started out bitter and resentful had made a shift to feeling more hopeful. Others, who had felt powerless, gained a sense of control over their lives. This exercise was a profound reminder that our words truly impact our beliefs, which then influence our attitudes, and ultimately produce our outcomes. I wonder which other aspects of our lives could benefit from a similar degree of intentionality?

> 'It's hard to learn that we don't leave the best part of ourselves behind back in the dugout or the office. We own what we learned back there, the experience and the growth are grafted into our lives And when we exit, we can take ourselves along. Quite gracefully.'

– Ellen Goodman (Pulitzer Prize Recipient)

Self-awareness and culture

Nicholas Wai

The **Australian Chamber Orchestra** (ACO) has been one of my favourite orchestras ever since I first saw them perform in Sydney. Later on, I had the chance to attend a string quartet masterclass delivered by Richard Tognetti of the ACO of the Australian Chamber Orchestra (ACO) at the Hong Kong Academy of Performing Arts. I was quite looking forward to seeing Richard teaching and inspiring the next generation of musicians in Hong Kong, and was pleasantly surprised that I also learned something about culture – not just from an art perspective, but from a social one as well.

Richard comes from a culture in which people are expected to have an opinion and it is OK to voice it. He thus conducted his masterclass with the assumption that the students knew what they were doing and asked them questions about their playing, whether they were happy with something, and how they could improve on it. The students were caught off guard by this method of 'teaching' and didn't know how to respond. I think they probably came from an environment in which a teacher would tell them what they did wrong and how they should have done it.

Richard did have to do a bit of that to get things started, when he reminded the students of the need to 'breathe as one' – to not only play individually but also to play together. Once they were able to apply this, the quartet sounded so different! As their self-confidence grew, the students began to offer their opinions more freely, and thus improved even more quickly. Not only were they more in tune with each other's playing, but they also became more self-aware. I saw a parallel with coaching: when we take on the responsibility for becoming more self-aware, we naturally take on the responsibility for improving ourselves. We are all experts at being ourselves, and we know what needs to be done when we are not performing at a standard acceptable to us.

On another level, the masterclass also helped me to understand culture more intimately. I now see the quartet as a microcosm of our society, a group that needs to operate in concert at a basic level to function properly. Within the quartet, the players have individual roles and responsibilities, and each needs to let their strengths and personalities shine in order to make beautiful music. In our society we have our common ideals, which include things like equality, safety, and the rule of law, and on this foundation we as individuals can pursue our respective goals and dreams and thrive. I see self-awareness as an essential skill for determining the part of the culture we need to maintain in order for society to function, and on the other hand in helping us know ourselves better so we can decide where and how we can apply and develop our potential.

Action or non-action...
the way to empowerment

Wendela Wolters & Yvonne Thackray

Sometimes making a decision not to do something is the best option. When we think about the word 'action', we have a picture of movement, getting something 'done'. But often, staying away or not doing something (for someone else), can have a much greater effect than simply jumping into action. Let me illustrate this with an example, which is taken from healthcare, but could also have parallels within any organization.

Over the last two decades, nursing theory has evolved from treating patients as people who were to be 'nursed' back into proper health to empowering patients to take the necessary steps to recovery themselves by providing them with assistance and knowledge. The nurse's role has broadened to include evaluating the patients' ability to handle health challenges. By being empathetic rather than sympathetic helps the nurse to remain autonomous, and this has became just as important as acting professionally in emergencies. In this situation, both the patient and the nurse are empowered to have more control in their respective personal and professional lives.

'Empowerment is not giving people power, people already have plenty of power, in the wealth of their knowledge and motivation, to do their jobs magnificently. We define empowerment as letting this power out.'[8]

For this reason action does not simply equate to 'staying away' from action. This process of empowering also demands

---

8 Blanchard *et al.* (1994) *Empowerment Takes More Than a Minute.*

a very different view of managing responsibility. Traditionally, a nurse had to responsibly judge the appropriate level of care when providing medical assistance to the patient. This often led the patient to enter an adapted state of helplessness in which they gradually lost the initiative and became increasingly dependent on their caregivers. (Note that some people are more vulnerable to this than others. People with a pessimistic explanatory style, who see negative events as permanent – 'it is not in my power to change' – are most likely to suffer from this mindset.)

The extent to which people believe they have power over events in their lives is reinforced through certain beliefs. Julian B. Rotter, one of the eminent psychologists of the 20th century, referred to this as 'locus of control'[9]. A person with an internal 'locus of control' believes that he or she can influence events and outcomes, while someone with an external 'locus of control' blames outside forces for everything – they feel they have no control over events and become passive.

Through the process of empowering all the responsibility belongs to the individual – this can be both a blessing and a curse depending where along the continuum of the 'locus of control' you are during that moment. However, empowerment is not an individual act even though it is about the individual; it is often an act between two people. A wise individual (whether a nurse, doctor, manager, parent, or coach) who is there to create the space for the process to begin must carefully judge when to 'act' or 'not act', and then provide positive reinforcements which will hopefully give the recipient confidence in their actions, giving them more control over their situation, and further motivating them to continue on the journey. And when they have achieved that state, both parties must take action and release each other from each other's agreement (formal or informal) until another challenge arises. This is the way to empowerment!

---

9 [website] *The social learning theory of Julian B. Rotter* | *psych.fullerton.edu*

CHAPTER 3

AWARENESS OF TIME

Kilometer 999: the concept of time

Charlotte Rydlund

Time and planning was a recurring theme in the first month after my geographical relocation. Time can have many meanings, connotations, and contexts. During this period, the context was personal, social and in business. Personally, time meant meeting deadlines. (The international move was a deadline, submitting administrative paperwork was a deadline.) Socially, time meant finding opportunities to see good friends before leaving and re-learning what time meant for people in Nova Scotia, Canada compared to Switzerland. From a business point of view, time meant planning and conducting meetings across multiple time zones, organizing logistics and preparing media packages for the cross-country scuba-diving expedition called CANADIVE, which my husband and I had founded.

The CANADIVE expedition emerged from our decision to relocate geographically, after completing outplacement coaching. I had realized that while moving, we could also do something good along the way – in a sense give back – whilst doing something we loved. Our intention was to mobilize local communities across Canada to help us collect underwater trash and debris at 99 dive sites over a four-month period (see www.canadive.org). This was the mission we had set for ourselves.

Because of the many things going on, timing and planning were vital. Here are my four top tips that I learned from this experience:

- **Prioritize.** When many things are going on at once, taking the time to prioritize has been crucial. Prioritizing has involves planning for the day, the week, and even the month ahead, and making choices of what will be priority 1, 2 and 3. Not everything can be priority 1, especially when there are hard deadlines – such as when the moving company is coming and when the flights are booked.

- **Be intentional.** Being intentional means sticking to the priorities you set while being flexible (see next point). It does not necessarily mean that everything will go according to plan, but at least any action you take is an intentional (actively chosen) one as opposed to a non-intentional one.

- **Remain flexible.** In any endeavour, things happen that you could not have foreseen. For example: I booked a taxi to take my husband and I to the airport along with 8 large and 2 small suitcases. I asked for a very large vehicle, and they showed up with a Toyota Prius (definitely not big enough!). Luckily we booked with plenty of time to spare, so they managed to send another vehicle and we still made our flight, but this was a minor hiccup in our overall plan.

- **Have fun.** It is easy for some (myself included) to be so focused on following a plan that every hiccup creates a sense of stress (like the Prius experience). I keep reminding myself that this is all part of the adventure of my transition, and to take all the experiences (planned or not) as an opportunity to learn and to enjoy the moment.

Multitasking: myth or fact?

Yvonne Thackray

Multitasking is a useful and extremely powerful skill for monitoring multiple sources of data in our information-saturated lives – for example, data mining, following an unfolding event, co-ordinating a group of people, or just looking for inspiration or entertainment. The act of multitasking is much like scanning. However, it isn't the same as giving a complex task your complete attention – or allowing yourself to engage and connect deeply with the place you are in, the task, and the people you are sharing it with. Imagine what you might be missing participating in!

p
a
y
i
n
g

a
t
t
e
n
t
i
o
n

Multitasking: myth or fact?

'Multitasking' is a word we have taken on board to describe our efforts to respond to the many pressing demands on our time. It's been glorified as a 'mark of mastery' in the modern age to be able to perform more than one task at a time.

Reality: Research from many neurologists and psychologists are showing that human brains are not built to multitask. The brain actually switches rapidly between tasks, and task-switching is an expensive habit that requires extra processing power and reduces efficiency.

The Evidence

Time to Finish

Studies from the Uni. of California and Microsoft have shown that it takes between 15-25 mins for our brain to recover from interruptions.

Productivity

HBR reports that productivity goes down by as much as 4% as the brain loses momentum when switching between tasks.

IQ

Distracted people experience a 10-point drop in their IQ – the equivalent of losing a full night of sleep. (Study carried out by Institute of Psychiatry for Hewlett Packard)

Stress

A Uni. of Washington study shows it adds stress to our environment. And according to psychologists it can negatively affect our relationships.

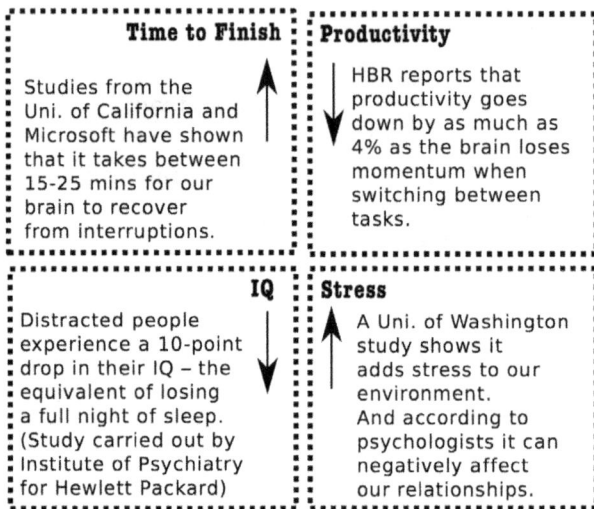

Factor in Personality

Extroverts are better at handling information overload as they focus on their goal. They process a lot of short-term information rapidly without being distracted or overstressed. Extroverts prioritize speed over accuracy and are more likely to make an increasing number of mistakes as they go. They tend to abandon a problem when it seems too difficult or frustrating.

Introverts are more reflective and focussed on monitoring how the task is progressing. They prefer to observe than participate in social dynamics, and so use up a lot of cognitive capacity. Introverts prioritize accuracy over speed. They think before they act, digest information thoroughly, stay on task longer, and give up less easily.

TIPS TO HANDLE MULTIASKING

Turn off interruptions

Book meeting times with yourself at work

Focus on what's important

Hire a coach

Multitasking is the art of paying attention

Taking the time to cultivate presence

Naomi Dishington

When life's Big Moments occur, as they are apt to do, you might intuitively know you need to do something called 'being present' – but maybe you aren't sure what that actually means or how it would help you. You might also suspect that whatever 'being present' means, it isn't something you can gulp down like an energy drink for a turbo-blast of enlightenment.

So what *does* it mean when we talk about 'being present', and why is it especially helpful in important situations like a job interview, a child's school performance, or a business negotiation? For starters, it involves being focused. Blocking out distractions. Actively listening. Being aware of your breath. Becoming fully engaged with the person(s) in front of you. Most times, it involves showing up in service of another, giving that person the gift of your full attention.

What if we started to think about developing presence like exercising our muscles? Both require a level of intentionality, repetition and practice. You can't realistically hope to be present and confident in big, impactful moments if you haven't spent time cultivating presence in the smaller, less significant moments.

So how can you begin? Working with a coach is a good place to start, because coaches are trained in the skill of slowing down and tuning out distractions, and can model 'being present' for you. In addition, your coach can help you become more attuned to and aware of your own reactive situations. Once you identify your triggers, you can implement small steps to become more present in those situations. As the saying goes, 'Being mindful is not difficult to do; it is difficult to remember to do'[10]. A coach provides some accountability as you learn to remember.

I recently discussed this topic with Andrea St. George, an Emotional Intelligence Coach[11] and author of *With Love in My Heart*. Her advice on learning to become present is to start small. Very small. She suggests practicing presence while brushing your teeth! Bring laser focus to your senses. How does each tooth feel? What about the gums? How does the toothpaste smell? What do you taste? How do your teeth look in the mirror? What sound is made by the brushing? According to St. George, no matter who you are, you'll never be fully present in the Big Moments if you don't learn to focus your attention on the sensations involved in something as basic and routine as the brushing of your teeth.

Once you've developed a bit of stamina in being present, you can begin to apply the tools while in traffic, or standing in line at the grocery store, and so on. Then you may find yourself flexing your presence muscles more often. Perhaps you'll need them in your challenges as a working mom, or during interpersonal conflicts, or while negotiating the purchase of a new home. The idea is to build up slowly and continue to practice until eventually you will have access to an inner reservoir of peace when you need it most.

Some might find this topic a bit vague, and wonder why cultivating presence is so important. Where's the benefit? My answer would be that it's about building a strong mental core, in much the same way that we try to build a strong physical core. The centre of our body holds us together and provides a base for myriad movements. Likewise, cultivating presence opens up access to other traits, such as confidence, authenticity, patience, love, and compassion. At its best, it is a way of offering ourselves fully to those around us. Spiritual author Henri Nouwen puts it this way: 'In a time so filled with methods and techniques designed to change people, to influence their behaviour, and to make them do new things and think new thoughts, we have lost the simple but difficult gift of being present to each other'[12].

---

10 Sharon Salzberg, *Real Happiness: The Power of Meditation.*

11 [website] *www.andreastgeorge.blogspot.com*

12 Nouwen *et al.* (2000) *Compassion: A Reflection on the Christian Life.*

Dealing with information overload and staying present

Wendela Wolters

Surrounded by the rolling hills of the beautiful French Normandy, our guesthouse on an organic farm provided us with the perfect environment for winding down after a busy year. But not before we experienced some anxiety brought on by digital withdrawal!

Our guesthouse had no internet connection, and on top of that our Dutch telecom company had trouble connecting our phones to the local network. We were on our own – isolated, cut off from business, news, family and friends, and even the media frenzy surrounding the birth of the royal baby!

It took some time getting accustomed to being disconnected from the digital world, and I found myself wondering if I missed something important. But I adjusted after a few days and started to work on my pile of books that had been waiting to be read for far too long. After a wonderful week we left the farm, the telephone company solved its communication problems, and we came home to be greeted by pile of newspapers. I went through all of them to make sure I hadn't missed anything.

Skimming through the news, I came across a tragic story: Carsten Schloter, CEO of a Swiss telecom company, was found dead, and a suicide note was found with his body[13]. Following a divorce in 2009, he had begun to feel overwhelmed by the enormous avalanche of information he had to tackle daily. During

13 [website] *'Swisscom chief executive Carsten Schloter who committed...'* | *Independent.co.uk*

a convention in Interlaken he said he was '...not wanting to live in a world where it was impossible to find a quiet space due to the continuous stream of new information...' For a CEO of a large telecom company this was quite a surprising statement!

Manfred Kets de Vries, clinical Professor of leadership development at INSEAD and also a psychoanalyst, states that many leaders in politics, healthcare and education suffer from Internet addiction disorder (IAD)[14]. They are addicted to their inbox and have great difficulty finding a balance between action and reflection.

Carsten Schloter was a charismatic and popular boss known for his enormous dedication and passion for the company. But tragically, at some point it became impossible for him to find that balance, that quiet space.

According to professor Kets de Vries, the emergence of the Internet has brought about some of the biggest changes to the lives of people in senior positions since the time of the Romans. Dealing with this avalanche of information is not always easy. He advises top managers to let an assistant handle the inbox and have a weekly meeting about 4-5 priority mails.

To find a balance between action and reflection it is important to give our brains some rest, for it is in that quiet time that we come up with our best decisions!

Here are some tips from psychologist Lucy Palladino[15] which can make it easier to find that balance:

- **Schedule a break regularly.** I find it very refreshing to do something that is the opposite of what I was doing. I try to alternate brainwork with a no-brainer like taking a walk or playing with my dog.

- **Set a limit:** The Internet can eat up your time, and before you know it an hour has passed. Limit how long you scan for information, and focus on high-quality sources.

---

14 Kets de Vries, Manfred, (2006) *The Leader on the Couch: a Clinical Approach to Changing People and Organizations.*

15 [website] *Lucy Jo Palladino, Ph.D | http://www.lucyjopalladino.com*

- **Keep your virtual and physical space clutter-free.** If you regularly organize and updated your files, it becomes much easier to handle the information overflow. Keep an eye out for helpful apps and programs, they can make a difference.

I hope that these tips are useful for you. Give your brain a breather and enjoy the beautiful day!

Sometimes the devil is in...
the preparations

Nicholas Wai

As in any relationship, both coach and client have an interest in finding out if their partnership will work. From the client's perspective, this may involve researching the coach's qualifications and expertise, his or her methods and preferences, and also his or her background and experience. From the coach's perspective, this may involve finding out about the client's issues, organisational context, and the readiness for coaching. To this end, a 'chemistry' meeting will usually be held before a coaching engagement, both to explore the factors mentioned above, and more importantly, to see if they will be a good 'fit' for each other.

I had the pleasure of being invited to one such meeting, and despite having been to quite a few before, I still felt a bit anxious about it. The meeting was with a potential client based in Hong Kong, but introduced to me by a coaching consultancy in the US. This is actually quite common especially for multinational clients, who tend to source their coaching needs via consultancies they are working with at headquarters, who in turn maintain a list of coaches in major cities around the world who share their values and practices.

No two chemistry meetings are exactly the same, and this one was different in that the prospect was an expatriate senior manager who had not worked with an executive coach before, and who would be meeting with a number of coaches before choosing one. Despite these circumstances, what I had control over was how I prepared for such a meeting. This was both calming and reassuring, and through visualization I was able to present my best face at the meeting and be present and fully engaged with the client. I think the meeting went quite well. We established a rapport a few minutes after shaking hands. We discussed the client's situation, I outlined my experience and view on coaching, and together we explored how a typical coaching engagement is organised and managed, how outcomes are measured (which depends very much on the context), and also shared our experiences in living and working in different countries.

So what did I do to prepare for the meeting? There were five steps to my preparation:

1. I reviewed the coaching models and tools I had learned and highlighted those that might be relevant for this engagement.

   - Although I was already very familiar with this material, it was still beneficial to review it in the context of a particular project.

2. I studied the profile of the client's organisation and also the bio of the prospective client supplied by the consultancy (supplemented by other information I managed to find online).

   - This helped me form a picture of the environment which the client operated in and also the client's past experience, which would have shaped his mindset and behaviours. However, this was just an overview, as I wanted to stay open-minded during the meeting.

3. I came up with different possible scenarios and prepared responses to each.

   - By running through the different questions that were likely to be asked and various possible scenarios, as well as my likely responses and reactions, I was not only better prepared but felt more confident that I would be able to handle them.

4. I visualised the meeting.

   - This not only helped me to familiarize myself with the scenarios, but also made me more aware of my likely thoughts and feelings, thus enabling me to feel more in control.

5. While preparing for the meeting and during the meeting itself, I reminded myself that this was a learning experience.

- Of all the steps I took to prepare for this meeting, I feel that this was the most important. By assuming a 'learning' rather than a 'fixed' mindset (as detailed in Carol Dweck's book *Mindset*, I was more able to keep an open mind and see options and learning opportunities rather than focusing on the 'right way' and what I might have been lacking. I was able to just be myself and be confident in the meeting. Although anxiety may come up again in the future, I know that with preparation, I will be able to centre myself and be ready for any opportunities when they arise.

Mindfulness: the Western answer to living in the present

Wendela Wolters

Participating intimately in life as it is unfolding and being fully aware of whatever is happening in the present moment, without judgment, is a different way of inhabiting the present moment. Being present and mindful is an important concept in many spiritual traditions, including Buddhism, Christianity, Hinduism and Taoism, but this idea has also expanded beyond its spiritual roots. Mindfulness has recently become a mainstream concept in the West and is being applied in a variety of contexts, including medicine, neuroscience, psychology and education. Many leading business schools, including Stanford and INSEAD, have begun incorporating mindfulness and meditation into their curricula to prepare students for learning to cope with the stress of daily life, and physicians are prescribing training in mindfulness to help people deal with stress, pain and illness and to improve emotional well-being.

Before I started practicing mindfulness techniques, I hadn't realized how busy I was with rehearsing, worrying about the future, and rehashing my life. It just went on and on, in a never-ending cycle, leaving little space for creativity or playfulness. We have 70,000 thoughts each day[16], most of them the same as the day before... and the day before. (I always wondered how they counted the thoughts?)

---

16 [website] *Bruce Davis, Ph.D.: 'There are 50,000 Thoughts Standing...' |* *Huffington Post*

This knowledge motivated me to continue my 8-week course[17]. Sometimes it felt uncomfortable, I felt restless and jumpy. Observing my own thoughts was sometimes quite confrontational! But as I learned to integrate the practice into my daily life I gradually became more at peace, and coping with stressful situations became easier.

As the ancient Buddhist Dhammapada begins, 'Mind is the forerunner of all...conditions. Mind is their chief; and they are mind-made'. This statement makes it clear that paying attention to, or being mindful of, your own mind is of the utmost importance. It is said that the intention is the crux of all action – that our intention shapes our thoughts, words and deeds.

I would like to end this segment with some fresh food for thought; read over the following progression a couple of times and take a moment to reflect on it:

- Intention shapes our thoughts and words.

- Thoughts and words mould our actions.

- Thoughts, words, and actions shape our behaviours.

- Behaviours sculpt our bodily expressions.

- Bodily expressions fashion our character.

- Our character hardens into what we look like.

---

17 In a study that appeared in the January 30 issue of *Psychiatry Research: Neuroimaging,* a team led by Massachusetts General Hospital (MGH) researchers reported the results of their study, the first to document meditation-produced changes over time in the brain's grey matter. Their research indicated that participating in an 8-week mindfulness meditation program appears to make measurable changes in brain regions associated with memory, sense of self, empathy and stress.

Invoke your presence in the present

Yvonne Thackray

'Invoke the presence of your Presence in the present'

– E.J. Gold

I**t's challenging** to write about presence – it's like trying to find a needle in a haystack! Where does one start? Or how does one end? Where's the thread? Where's the needle? By frantically searching for 'it', what was I missing – the point?

There are subtle differences when talking about presence – with a little 'p', presence is part of time, the here and now, and with a capital 'P', Presence is a part of the emerging future – the question is, how do they interrelate? Living systems i.e. you, me, the trees, the weather system, our ecosystem, create themselves and continually grow and adapt to changing conditions. However, we have been trained to believe that the whole is made up of separate components that can be replaced or repaired, to complete a singular known goal. This pure rational thinking is useful when we speak about inanimate objects like machines because the specifications and functions of each component are quite clear, but it's not the optimal way to think about natural living systems. Johann Wolfgang von Goethe, the German writer and scientist, argued over 200 years ago that we need to ask more insightful questions about nature because the whole is something that is dynamic and living and which continually comes into being 'in concrete manifestations', whilst a part is a manifestation of the whole rather than its component – neither can exist without the other. The part and the whole are vital. Hence, without being present we may miss Presence in the present!

And therein lies the point. To be present in Presence in the present we need to be aware of its existence and the interrelatedness between the part and the whole. For example, each of us is a unique individual (*whole*) and we can develop in different ways (*part*) to help us grow into our best selves. When we interact with another person or group of individuals, we become a *part* of another *whole* and our social identity, congruent with our core identity, matches the surrounding environment. When our personal and social identity is in balance we are normally present because we have a sense of calmness, purpose and direction. However, most people spend the majority of their time passively tackling conflicts with others and within ourselves, and with the rapid pace we now live at, it has become harder to find the time to cultivate presence in one's life. Thus, rather than tackling the *whole* at once, we need to consciously take the time to focus on the *parts* which make up our whole, or even the subdivisions of those parts that are manageable, to make small but positive changes. And when we do this, something new emerges.

Sensing these shifts requires awareness: as it requires noticing the movement from a state of negative emotion to that of calmness or peace or productivity, for example. And this awareness comes from being able to register experiences without prejudice by utilizing all of our senses whilst we:

- Suspend our assumptions/negative chatter (which takes practice).

- Allow ourselves to see alternative and/or emerging events, contents, patterns etc.

- Observe what's actually happening from all perspectives by slowing down and taking the necessary time to absorb what is going on.

- Listen actively and empathically.

- Retreat and reflect to process all of the above and allow them to connect with the bigger picture.

With time, Presence emerges from within us to make meaning and allow us to reconnect with the external world (the whole) with such a level of clarity that decision-making is needed because the appropriate action is obvious. That awareness, that shift, is subtle but visceral, and indicates that one is Present. By recognising that presence and taking the action that naturally flows from it, we are in our Presence.

CHAPTER 4

TAKING ACTION STARTS WITH A FIRST STEP

Kilometer 2,000: in the action

Charlotte Rydlund

With all the planning and preparation completed, the CANADIVE Expedition finally started. Finally it was actually happening, it really was happening. For me this was so important, because it meant the pathway to my career transition was officially open!

I must admit, action felt good, really really good! While there were many reasons why it felt good to *do* something, the one on the top of my list was that what I was doing felt absolutely right. No regrets, no second-guessing, no faltering in my determination. Although I had noticed this feeling before, continuing to feel that what I was doing was right for me gave me an extra adrenaline kick that energized me even more.

The second reason why being in action felt good was because when you do something, you get results. In my case, the CANADIVE expedition was about mobilizing local communities and divers across Canada to collect underwater trash and debris. So, in terms of results, it felt good to have almost 600 lbs/270 kg of trash collected, to be welcomed and encouraged by local divers and communities, and to be invited to interview with CBC Radio. These were tangible results that were consequences of action.

The third reason why action felt good – and this one might sound strange to some – was because there was always an element of the unexpected. When we dove to collect marine debris[18] we never knew what we were going to find. We had found unusual items like a rotary telephone, a car radio case, and a glass bottle

---

18 Marine debris definition (Wikipedia): Human-created waste that has deliberately or accidentally been released in a lake, sea, ocean or waterway.

from the 1950s. Like with any action, you could plan and prepare to perfection, but there was always going to be a small pinch of the unexpected that would add a twist to your plans.

These points were written while on the ferry between Newfoundland and Nova Scotia:

- **Embrace the unexpected.** I had mentioned this point previously (have fun) but it was important for me to (re)state it. The unexpected is the part of life that you cannot plan for. The unexpected does happen, for better or for worse, and so far it just added to the adventure. It was unexpected that we would be invited by the Mayor of the town of Holyrood to do a cleanup dive there. It was also unexpected that a casual conversation with someone in the local dive shop would lead to several days of activities and the forging of new friendships.

- **Keep a learning mindset.** Keeping an open 'learner' mindset is invaluable. Keeping a learner mindset for me means that you remain open-minded and curious. I learned what it sounded like when our muffler decided to drop off on the highway, and how to change a timing belt on our truck. I also learned how to shuck fresh scallops, and what it was like to be interviewed live on the radio.

- **Keep your 'to do' list short.** As always, I had my daily 'to do' list, but when on the road, it was helpful to spread out what I wanted to do. Especially because of unexpected events (see point 1); if there are too many items on your 'to do' list, then adventure and learning can turn into stress (or at least, it could in my case). I kept my 'to do' list to a daily maximum of 3. One day I had these three tasks : i) do an interview with CBC radio; ii) do a cleanup dive; iii) make sure the moose steaks we were given by our Newfoundland friends were thawed for dinner. Luckily I did not have more on my list, because later that afternoon we spent four hours walking along the beautiful beach and spontaneously continued our debris cleanup on the shore (and carried all 59 kg/132 lbs of it back to the recycling depot). Another day was: i) drive 4.5 hours in time to make the ferry, and get some good footage of the route; ii) write this segment; and iii) contact dive shops for the upcoming stops on our route in New Brunswick and Quebec.

The importance of goals (and knowing when to give up!)

Yvonne Thackray

Having goals gives us a sense of purpose, as they help define what's important to us and identify actions for keeping us on track. They can be any size – extra-small, small, medium, large, or extra-large. It doesn't matter – they have to mean something for us to want to commit time, resources and courage towards fulfilling them. Have fun making goals and then following through – it's been proven that you can find happiness along the way! Also, when circumstances change and the goal no longer fits you, don't hesitate to give it up. Failure is just a part of life. Accept it, forgive yourself and move on. Learn from the experience and it can open you up to be more creative, innovative, spontaneous and confident in your next endeavour!

Importance of having goals

Making Goals is vital for:

Giving a sense of meaning
Happiness – it's strongly associated with making progress to personally relevant goals
Self regulation – Being able to define an acceptable performance level

Why we have...

- Organise time
- Make decisions
- Prioritize resources
- Measure life progress
- Learn new skills
- Develop sense of meaning

G
O
A
L
S

How we categorise...

Outcome goals:
Environmentally controlled, and can be demotivating
Performance goals:
In your control and associated with higher performance
Process goals:
Performance sub-goals
Learning goals:
Situations where you have little or no expertise

How we express...

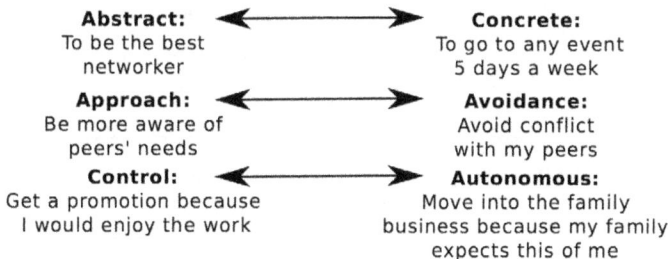

Abstract: ←——————→ **Concrete:**
To be the best
networker
To go to any event
5 days a week

Approach: ←——————→ **Avoidance:**
Be more aware of
peers' needs
Avoid conflict
with my peers

Control: ←——————→ **Autonomous:**
Get a promotion because
I would enjoy the work
Move into the family
business because my family
expects this of me

Success in completing... GOALS

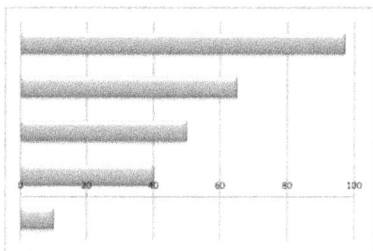

97% Have a specific accountability action plan with the accountability partner

65% Commit to the plan with an accountability partner

50% Plan how to do it

40% Decide when to do it

10% Have an idea

Data: Wiseman, R. (2004) *Did You Spot the Gorilla?*

having goals

g
i
v
i
n
g
-
u
p
•
g
o
a
l
s
•

Knowing when to give up a goal

Fear of failure is the biggest factor which holds people back from taking action. We stand to lose more in the event of failure, so fear kicks in to protect our fragile self esteem. Preventative strategies include:

Self-handicapping:
Creating conditions to explain or excuse a potential failure
Defensive pessimism:
Consciously setting extremely low expectations for the future
Procrastination:
Putting off overwhelming or unenjoyable work

Take courage and accept that failure is inevitable

Be brave and recognise when it's time to give up on a goal.

Abandoning a goal is wise when:

- **Rate of progress** isn't sufficient
- Circumstances have **changed**
- The goal is **no longer relevant**

Research evidence points to 'giving up' as a human strength! Giving up a goal is better than wasting effort, as it stops you from being stuck in no-mans land where you're unable to move forward and never fully disengage from the task.

How to commit to worthwhile goals

- **Make it fun and appealing, add beauty**
- **Closely examine which underlying values are driving you**
- **Build in failure – purposely make mistakes and see what emerges**
- **Focus on progress & celebrate small successes along the way**
- **Have a learning mindset**
- **Hire an accountability coach**

Pathway to sustainable change

Naomi Dishington

Most **coaches** would probably agree that bringing a client to a point of actionable awareness is a key coaching competency. The idea of moving to action is so central to coaching that many models build decisional work into the conclusion of each session. They use questions such as:

- 'What will you do with this new learning?'

- 'What one change are you determined to make today?'

- 'What are you willing to give up now in order to get what you want later?'

It is precisely this focus on action and accountability that differentiates coaching from traditional approaches used in therapy.

Because action lies at the heart of coaching, coaches may mistakenly measure their skill levels by the rate at which their clients act. It could be tempting for a coach to gauge success by the client's initial commitment to change, but research shows that '[Sustainable] change actually happens in a series of predictable stages rather than in one giant leap'[19]. A coach should feel free to celebrate a moment of discovery or a new initiative with her client, but she should also remember that the least successful outcomes occur when we expect 'giant leaps'.

James Prochaska[20], a prominent researcher from the University of Rhode Island in the US, collected data on over 6,000 cases of

19 Zenger *et al.* (2010) *The Extraordinary Coach: How the Best Leaders Help Others Grow.*

20 [website] *Transtheoretical model | Wikipedia, the free encyclopedia*

addiction and came to the simple yet powerful conclusion that change is not one moment, nor one decision, but rather a series of successive steps. He identified key stages in the change process, which are covered in detail in John Zenger's *The Extraordinary Coach: How the Best Leaders Help Others Grow*.

Prochaska concluded that counsellors (or coaches) who saw their task as moving someone in a giant leap had the lowest rates of success. Those with the greatest success rates saw their role as helping people to move from one stage to the next (precontemplation, contemplation, preparation, action and maintenance), while always showing great respect for where the person was in the process of changing. Although Prochaska's research focused on addictions, the concepts are easily transferable to coaching, and his Stages of Change model is useful in all areas of human development, including parenting, education, and management.

If coaches bring grand expectations of change to coaching engagements, they risk subtly cueing their clients that they're waiting for a big 'A-ha!' moment. But such moments can't be forced, and both the coach and the client may become discouraged if an ambitious change doesn't stick.

The role of a coach is to manage and facilitate while reframing expectations, thus allowing growth to happen; however, lasting change doesn't happen quickly or in great leaps. Perhaps our best course of action is to invite clients to move toward actionable awareness while simultaneously emphasising that taking small steps is the surest path to sustainable change.

A coin has two sides

Nicholas Wai

U nderstanding who we are helps us to see how and why we take certain actions. As coaches, there are many tools available to help us understand different personalities, and one of the more popular ones is the enneagram[21]. This model states that there are nine inter-related personality types, with each having a particular set of tendencies and behaviours driven by different inner needs including the need to be perfect, loved, successful, special, wise, safe, free, powerful, or peaceful. I learned about enneagrams many years before I became a coach, but I recently had the opportunity to study under Dr Jerry Wagner. His background as a clinical psychologist and psychotherapist added a different perspective and further depth to my practical understanding of the theory.

What I found interesting about Dr Wagner's take on the subject is how he manages to combine his psychology background with the ancient knowledge of the enneagram to map out the development of each personality type based on their values and what ideals they hold. He theorises that by pursuing some ideals instead of others, we form our preferences and thus personalities. Specifically, we each hold some values to be important to us, such as being industrious, fair, creative, or intelligent. These are all worthwhile ideals in themselves, and there is nothing to prevent us from pursuing them all at the same time.

As human beings we are very good at focusing on values and actions that we hold dear, a legacy from our hunter-gatherer origins. These preferences mean that instead of holding each

---

21 [website] *The Enneagram Spectrum of Personality Styles | Jerome P. Wagner*

ideal with equal regard, we tend to develop our own likes and dislikes, which in turn inform our behaviours. These preferences, as they are based on ideals, motivate us to do many good things for ourselves and the people around us. However, when we choose to pursue our preferences at the expense of other ideals, we may lose balance and overreact. This overreaction is the trait which some refer to as the dark side of a particular personality type.

For example, a person with an enneagram type 3 personality is usually described as very goal- and result-oriented, pursuing the ideal of being productive and industrious. This in itself is a very good thing, as without type 3 people the world would not be as progressive, advanced or prosperous as it is today. However, when such a person is narrowly focused on such a pursuit with little regard to the other ideals such as love and fairness, we may see the person manipulating others or cutting corners in order to get his or her way.

Thus we can see that an ideal can be a force of good, but if pursued exclusively it can also be destructive. By the same token, things which we might see as a hindrance to us (such as being overly cautious, for a type 6 person) can be beneficial as times when being cautious and considerate is called for. In my coaching, I have utilised enneagram theory to help clients pursue their goals. It enables me to reframe their perceived weaknesses as context- and degree-dependent strengths (for example, for a type 9 person whose ultimate ideal is peace, his or her difficulty in saying 'no' could be reframed as a strength when mediation or team-based collaboration is called for).

There are many ideals worth pursuing, and enneagram theory is not only about understanding our personalities. It is also about what ideals we choose to uphold over other equally-worthy ideals, all in pursuit of the ultimate goal of becoming a more developed, well-rounded, and worthwhile person.

Respect culture:
start by scratching the surface

Charlotte Rydlund

What is culture? It's such a broad topic that it's hard to know where to start. Culture can mean so many things, and has a different meaning or connotation for everyone. Culture can be a country's culture, a religion's culture, an organization's or company's culture. It can even be a family culture.

Culture is something that we interact with every day, both within our own culture (or comfort zone) and when learning about and discovering new cultures (by travelling to a new country or joining a new organization). The way we interact with people is influenced by our culture.

Do we shake hands when we meet? Or do we bow, hug, wave, or even look away? All of this depends on culture. Even a simple gesture like greeting someone makes you realize how important a role culture plays in our everyday lives.

Because culture is so ingrained in each of us in our own way, as long as you interact within your own cultural context, gestures like greeting or thanking someone comes naturally. However, when you start branching out you can quickly find yourself outside your comfort zone. When I was in Thailand, I remember being especially conscientious about showing respect when greeting or thanking someone. I tried to remember how to say *hello* and *thank you* in Thai (even if it was with a very poor accent). The same thing happened when I was in Kenya and Egypt. I wanted to show respect to the people and their culture.

Interacting with a different culture can open your eyes to new ways of doing things that you might never have thought of or tried otherwise. It can teach you new things about yourself. In fact, this is very similar to the experience of undergoing coaching.

Having a certain culture means you naturally see things in a certain way. It can be a combination of your national-religious-geographical and socioeconomic cultures, and of course your own personal perspective. As Anaïs Nin says, 'We don't see things as they are, we see them as we are.'[22]

When entering a coaching conversation it is possible that you might feel stuck or see only one way forward. This is similar to interacting within your own culture and within your comfort zone. When you interact with new cultures, you discover something new. A meaningful coaching conversation can help you learn something about yourself, discover possible blindspots, and preconceptions that are keeping you from getting un-stuck. Like discovering new cultures, coaching can help you gain a new perspective, and see new possibilities and ideas.

---

22 [website] *Anaïs Nin Quotes | BrainyQuote*

The properties of change:
what we know so far

Yvonne Thackray

Tackling change is something that we can take control of – or be plunged into, regardless of whether we want it or not. Change is inevitable, and we may recognise some of the signals that it is on the way – or we may not. Yet when the unexpected takes us by surprise, it provokes an emotional reaction that unsettles us. Emotions are indicators that help us assess what is to come. When we focus on our emotional state and assess all the incoming data, we make a decision about whether to take action. In extreme situations, if we recognise that our emotions are warning us of imminent danger, then we need to heed them and use them to help create a unique strategy to deal with the unexpected. This is what Daniel Kahneman, a recipient of the Nobel Prize in Economic Sciences, calls System 1 and System 2 thinking: 'System 1 is fast, intuitive and emotional; System 2 is slower, more deliberative, and more logical.' We have a tendency to focus on one more than the other, but when we harness both, we often create outcomes that surprise even ourselves.

Recent discoveries in neuroscience indicate that our brain has more than one hundred billion interconnected neurons, and they fire off in sequence to create an infinite number of patterns associated with specific mental functions e.g. recalling a past event or feeling pain or happiness. New discoveries are being made into how the mind and brain work together – as Dan Siegel (M.D.) points out, 'Mental activity stimulates brain firing as much as brain firing creates mental activity'. Each time we experience something, our neurons are activated, and through 'repetition, emotional arousal, novelty and the careful focus of attention, the synaptic linkages between the neurons strengthen, and that is how we learn from experiences'. Thus, if we want to make changes we need to focus our attention and create new patterns of neural firing to create new links, whether it's to master a new skill or change or reinforce a behaviour.

While acknowledging that we all have the capacity to take action and make changes, we must also be aware of other factors that can impede our progress: our character and the environment we live in. The rate at which we change needs to match with who we are and align with our values and identity in order to be sustainable. Some individuals can change more quickly than others because they have the confidence to live with uncertainty and chaos and the capacity to let go of the past, whilst others take longer to undergo personal transitions. The best thing is to change at the pace you feel comfortable with – after all, it is a very personal journey. We also need to have the discipline to help us in transition in the environment we live in. Here are some ways to stay motivated:

- Minimize access to those temptations that impede progress and keep away from bad situations.

- Have a support network that truly want the best for you and believes you have the potential to make changes.

- Create meaningful and manageable goals that focus on the now.

- As circumstances change, your goals should be modified or adapted to the change too – ongoing change can only be attained by sustained action.

CHAPTER 5

CHANNELING PRESENCE IN ALL ITS DIVERSITY

Kilometer 5,800: presence while on the road

Charlotte Rydlund

I had been on the road for several months, and was busier than I could remember. Wake up at 6am (or sometimes before) to complete a press release, pack up tent and gear, do at least one dive, drive five hours while writing a blog for CANADIVE and seeking out the next coffee shop along the road that has free Wi-Fi. That being said, every day was different. A different schedule, a different route, a different campground, a different dive site.

With all of the commotion that came with being in the middle of the action, I realized that 'being present' felt different and was more profound for me then than when I worked in a corporate environment.

Firstly, each day was so different – there was no set 'routine' like I used to have. Without a set routine, I found that I was naturally more present than I might have been on a normal Tuesday because my previous corporate life routine meant that I was often doing things on autopilot and was therefore not 100% present.

Secondly, I was more present because I didn't have 24-hour, 7-day-a-week internet access like I was used to. We had days where there was no cell phone coverage (only satellite phone) and where we passed only one coffee shop on the road that had free W-Fi during that entire day. At first it felt very abrupt, but I quickly adjusted to life in the unconnected world. I enjoyed the sunset as we drove along a wooded road (while keeping a lookout for moose and deer), and I noticed funny road signs, such as the one reading, 'Don't feed the bears, they may be dangerous'. I even started noticing the small things that I might not have paid attention to before because I was always checking my smartphone. Not being connected gave me time to actually *do something productive*, like process and think about my next blog, plan our next few days' itinerary, and prepare another press release – all without the constant distractions and interruptions that come with being online.

Thirdly, for me presence always comes with listening. Listening is as essential as a coach as it is for a scuba diver; *Co-Active Coaching*™ talks about three levels of listening; level 1 is with the self in the centre, level 2 is the client's words in the centre and level 3 is listening to the client in the centre while integrating signals from the holistic environment (body language, sounds in the background, voice and so on). I made a strong link in my mind between the three levels of listening and scuba diving. In scuba diving you need to be aware of yourself and your surroundings (the weather, the water, any boat traffic) and your dive buddy at all times. Whether it's constantly adjusting your air underwater so that you maintain buoyancy at depth, or picking up that the tide has turned or the current has increased (which means you might have to change your dive plan) or checking on your dive buddy to make sure they're OK – all of this requires constant listening, and adapting accordingly. You cannot *not* be present while scuba diving. You cannot *not* be present while coaching either.

A few things to think about on being present:

- **Notice when you're on autopilot.** That's the first step to practicing presence even in moments when you might daydream or withdraw from the situation (or just quickly check your email).

- **Take time to disconnect from the online world – totally.** This is why I felt that my being present in my transitory situation had really increased. Being disconnected from the online world was not actually a choice I made, but it came with the circumstances, and I appreciated the benefits.

- **Listen, listen, listen.** Even if you think you're listening, listen some more (at level 3 – holistic environment). The only thing that can happen is that you might see something from a new perspective (either below the water or above).

- **Get some distance and perspective.** Being busy means you're doing things (whether it's part of a routine, a habit (checking email) or something else). While on the road, and having been so busy in a non-routine way, being consciously present helped me keep an eye on the big picture while in a state of transition.

The price of stress and how to manage it

Yvonne Thackray

Stress is a natural part of life, and it is not possible to eliminate it entirely. Even experiencing happiness can cause stress – and what would life be without happiness? As Hans Selye (1974) states, 'Stress is the spice of life... Complete freedom from stress comes only in death'.

Stress can both have positive and negative effects in our life (see Charlotte Rydlund's career transition). We experience 'positive' stress (called eustress) when certain stressful situations and experiences provide us with a positive feeling of achievement, triumph, or exhilaration. Conversely, stress becomes distress (i.e. 'negative' stress) when we lose control and our sense of security is threatened. Recognising the difference between the two types of stress, and learning how to manage factors that cause us distress, will allow us to deal more effectively with challenges that life offers.

The price of stress and how to manage it

Definition: Stress is 'the adverse reaction people have to excessive pressure or other types of demand placed on them'.

What does that mean? Stress is a natural part of human functioning, but prolonged stress, and exposure to the chemicals associated with our flight/fight response can lead to ill-health and even death in extreme situations. Finding appropriate stress-management techniques to mitigate these excessive pressures will help you stay healthy and sane.

Stress vs. Pressure – Pressure is the situation, which the individual must adapt to. Stress comes from within the person, caused by the body's attempts to adapt to the situation.

THE FACTS

1. In the UK between April 2010 and March 2011 an estimated 1.2 million people said they were suffering from an illness caused or made worse by their work. Of these, 500,000 were new illnesses occurring in that year. **– Health and Safety Executive 2011**

2. 91% of adult Australians feel stress in at least one important area of their lives. Almost 50% feel very stressed about one part of their life. **– Lifeline Australia**

3. 80% of workers feel stress on the job – nearly half say they need help managing stress. 42% say co-workers need help. **– American Institute of Stress**

4. Workers put in a staggering 26 million extra hours in the workplace each day. 6 in 10 employees regularly work 1.5 hours overtime per day on average. Nearly 1 in 4 claim they work an extra 2-3 hours daily. 79% of these hours are unpaid, which is approx. £225 million of 'free' hours each day for employers. **– Aviva October 2011**

5. Approx. 13.7million working days lost annually in UK from work related illnesses costing approx. £28.3billion/yr. **– National Institute for Health and Clinical Excellence**

6. Stress levels in the workplace are rising, with 6 in 10 workers in major global economies experiencing increased workplace stress. China (86%) has the highest rise. **– The Regus Group**

managing

stress

m
a
n
a
g
i
n
g

s
t
r
e
s
s

HOW TO MANAGE COMMON STRESSES

Time Stress

Worrying about time or the lack of it to complete tasks; fear of failing to achieve something important; feeling trapped, unhappy or even hopeless.

1. Learn good time management skills.
2. Prioritize goals using Urgent/Important Matrix.
3. Learn how to create more time in your day.
4. Learn to say 'no' politely and assertively.

Anticipatory Stress

Stressed about the future, which be vague and undefined. Overall sense of dread about the future, worried that 'something will go wrong'.

1. Learn to meditate.
2. Work through the potential scenarios of the future, and visualise the situation going well repeatedly.
3. Learn how to overcome fear of failure.

Situational Stress

Being in scary situations that you have little or no control over, e.g. conflict, a loss of status, or rejection by your peers.

1. Learn to be more self-aware. Recognise the triggers (physical & emotional) which signal your response. Then learn how to manage them.
2. Learn effective conflict-resolution skills.

Encounter stress

Interacting with a certain individuals or groups of people, either because you do not like them or because they're unpredictable.

1. Develop greater emotional intelligence.
2. Recognise when you've reached your limit for interactions in the day.
3. Practice deep breathing exercises when you encounter these situations.
4. Develop empathy, a valuable coping skill for this type of stress.

How not to spend your whole day on Facebook

Nicholas Wai

No, I don't spend my whole day on Facebook, but whenever a deadline is fast approaching and a project needs some effort on my part to complete, I often find myself swinging between a state of flow, where I'm happily focusing and enjoying the task at hand, and procrastination, which includes checking Facebook, among other activities. With the deadline for completing this piece fast approaching, I found myself clearing out emails that have been sitting in my inbox for a few days, reading up on material for workshops that are scheduled a month away, and watching YouTube videos that could really be watched at any time but now! But that's when I stumbled onto Charles Duhigg's video on *big think*[23] and the *Good Life Project*[24].

You might have heard of his book, *Power of Habit*, which reminds us that we are all creatures of habit and have been ever since we were cave people. That's why in a stressful situation we make 'fight or flight' decisions almost instantaneously. Our brain automates many routine decision-making processes because our willpower is limited, and so we selectively use our time and spend it on four to five taxing tasks or decisions per day. New mindfulness-related techniques might enable us to build up our willpower, but changing our habits is still no easy task. Duhigg suggests that the best way to change our habits is by building new habits that overwrite the old ones.

---

23 [website] *How Not to Spend your Whole Day on Facebook | Big Think*
24 [website] *Charles Duhigg On the Power of Habit in Biz and Life ...*

Habits follow a process of cue-routine-reward. The key to understanding and changing a habit is to find out what the cues and rewards are in a particular habit loop, which we can do by recording and then alternating our routine for a few days. Take my procrastination example; it usually kicks in when I start feeling bored or anxious, and I try to relieve it by doing something that takes my mind off it, like cleaning the house or surfing the web. As I find comfort in such behaviours, the habit becomes stronger and more automatic. Even though I still manage to complete my actual tasks in the end, I usually have to go through several cycles of this habit, the procrastination loop, which can be very tiring.

To break this vicious cycle, I first have to recognise that I have this habit and that I don't want it to continue. To be successful, the key is not to abruptly stop the old habit, but to ease out of it by integrating my existing habit into the new habit that I want to start. Rather than denying myself any procrastination time, I turn it into a reward with 10 minutes of web-surfing for every 50 minutes of focused work. As I build this new habit, replacing the cue from a feeling of anxiety or boredom to that of satisfaction from completing my work, I can gradually extend my focused working time with a proportional increase in reward time. While I am still trying this out, I can say I'm already feeling much more motivated than before, as I move away from blaming myself for procrastinating to congratulating myself on starting a new habit!

Quietly reflecting and connecting with change

Yvonne Thackray

Change has always been and always will be that one constant in our lives, but the results of changes can either impact us head-on or at a glacial pace, without us even realizing that we are changing. It is often easier to pinpoint those momentous moments when we have undergone a drastic (and hopefully positive!) change, because these events are almost inevitably grand and dramatic in nature. However, taking the time to see how more gradual changes occurred, noticing those innocuous signs that are often hidden in plain sight, takes a bit of analysis, critical thinking, and reflection. It takes a quieter and more personal approach.

The question then becomes, 'How do we make more sense of those small changes?' We often take minor transitions for granted, yet it could be the accumulation of all those minor transitions that result in sustainable and significant changes that 'just feels right'. If every fibre and sensation in our mind and body agrees with it, and those who support us are aligned with us – it has become that mythical win-win-win situation. As you read this, you might be a bit cynical, which is fair enough, but I would like to ask you to take just a minute and think back to a moment when you experienced something, however big or small, that made you feel good. Take a deep breath, close your eyes and just enjoy that moment... Good work! (And even if you didn't bother, thank you for putting up with what I wrote!) Now, just think of all those small moments that pushed you forward to reach that moment, and consider how you behaved and the actions you took during those moments. You might have been aware, or you might not, but that's OK, because you are aware of them now.

If, after doing that quick reflection, you feel it might be worthwhile to take the time to record those changes, fleeting thoughts, connections and emotions that are part of our constant ongoing change, then I highly recommend taking the time to keep a diary or journal. It can be a time-consuming process, but it's important to have that clear idea of why you are doing it – whether to record past facts, to be creative, to measure progress, to vent, to share private moments, to formulate plans and ideas, to just enjoy writing – it could be for just one or any combination of those reasons. And, it's not necessary to write in the diary every single day – I think you can tell what my approach is! Write as much or as little as you want, because only you will be reading it – unless you choose to share your diary on- or offline. (I'm slightly old-fashioned and like to write down my thoughts with a pen on a page in a diary, with the occasional doodle.)

Then, at opportune or random moments, or after reflecting, take the time to read through your diary or extracts thereof. It will give you insights and perspectives on what's important to you. Taking action and reflecting on change at an individual level helps us create our personalized narrative of how we are doing both personally and socially. Taking the time to reflect could also help us ensure that we don't repeat the same mistakes and perhaps help us to formulate better actions in the future.

Like yoga, coaching is a practice in making choices

Nicholas Wai

I **have** been practicing yoga for several years now, but it is only recently that I have started to realise the true purpose of yoga: it is not about being able to maintain esoteric positions – it is actually all about breathing.

I was given this new insight by a new teacher at my yoga studio. Neil had been in Hong Kong for only a short time, but he has quickly established a reputation as a gifted teacher. Many other classes tended to be highly competitive, with students attempting to outdo each other by mastering ever more demanding positions, but in his *ashtanga* and *hatha* classes Neil would spend time explaining the essence of yoga instead, so we could better understand why we were doing a certain pose and what the main focus of that pose should be.

He explained that the purpose of any pose is to train ourselves to breathe deeply and comfortably, and that the poses put us in situations where we would normally breathe quickly and shallowly. It is only through practice, with a calm mind and grace that we can attain the Holy Grail of breath control.

Before this awareness, I have always had in the back of my mind the question, 'Why are we doing all these poses?' and thought if it was only about stretching and being more flexible, then it was a very slow process. Now it all made sense!

That led me to think about the similarities between yoga and coaching. The thing is, I think most people can do this if they force themselves – but doing something against our will equates to 'doing violence to ourselves' (to quote my favourite teacher, Professor Rao).

My yoga revelation helped me come to the conclusion that coaching is about supporting our clients to become more self-aware and make better choices by helping them think through the different alternatives and rationales, while recognising the values that naturally draw them to a certain choice, and putting that choice into practice

By practicing presence and making choices, we can honour our self-motivating values and natural strengths which will enable us to be better prepared for all the challenges that come our way in the adventure that is life. And quoting my favourite teacher again, we can be 'more invested in the process'.

Sharing amongst the like-minded, and beyond

Charlotte Rydlund

When I heard a CBC Radio segment discussing the 'share economy', I got curious about how fusing the human nature of sharing with commercial viability was revolutionising what sharing is about. According to Wikipedia, the share economy (also known as 'sharing' or 'collaborative economy') is 'an economic system built around the sharing of human and physical assets' which uses information technology to share goods and services. I was always aware of such companies, as I use them daily, but what truly struck me was how many companies' business plans are predicated on sharing. From Facebook and Twitter to AirBnB and Uber (and many more), these companies are successful because both the developers and users of the service want to share. They see a need that can be fulfilled by sharing, and as a consequence, these companies offer services or products that benefit others by sharing.

Isn't this one of the first things we learn growing up? Robert Fulghum wrote 'All I really need to know I learned in Kindergarten'[25], and the first one on the list is 'share everything'. Another well-used phrase is 'Sharing is caring'. Thanks to social media and the share economy, sharing has evolved from just a way for people to share what they think, feel and believe in, to also become a source of innovation, profit, and learning.

What is it about sharing that is so intrinsic to us as human beings? Whether it's dividing something with others or sharing a 'secret' (we all remember from kindergarten how big a thing that

25 Fulghum, R. (1990). *All I really need to know I learned in Kindergarten.*

was), or sharing ideas, knowledge, opinions, photos, or dreams. Why is it that we are compelled to share things we are passionate about? The fact that a lot of sharing now takes place online does not reduce the human instinct and desire to do so.

Sharing is not only about giving to others; it's also about what we choose to share of ourselves with the world. I watched Benjamin Zander's master class *Lessons for Music, Lessons for Life*, in which he worked with musicians to improve their playing. One comment he repeated several times was, 'It's not about you, it's about the audience and the story you want to share'. For the musicians this wasn't as obvious as one might expect, and it was amazing to see the transformation of these very talented musicians, whose performances improved dramatically. Their excitement and involvement visibly increased once they realized that 'it wasn't about them'.

Clearly the musicians were very talented in their field. Technically, they were experts. From my point of view, the comment, 'It's not about you' was the catalyst that enabled the musicians to go beyond their expertise and to focus instead on the art of storytelling that would open a dialogue and learning experience between the musician and the audience.

This as an extremely valid point, and equally useful outside the world of music. It's not about your expertise, but the story you tell and therefore how you 'show up' in the world. How might you choose to 'show up' – mentally, physically and emotionally – to tell the story you want to share? What is it you want to share with your 'audience' (be it your partner, your boss, your consumer or client, or a stranger)? How will sharing a part of yourself impact your audience? Choosing the story you tell is what makes your expertise unique.

Having worked in the corporate marketing world and in executive coaching, I see parallels in those fields as well. In marketing, how do you get a consumer to buy your product/ service instead of your competitor's, even if it's a commodity? It's the story you share that makes the difference, even if the product is very similar in functionality (expertise) to others on the market. It's the story you tell about the product/service that goes beyond the functionality (expertise) of the product and makes it unique and compelling for the 'audience'.

The share economy companies that I mentioned earlier are not necessarily offering something radically different from others, but it's how they 'show up' that makes them unique and draws in an 'audience'– revolutionizing what sharing is about.

When it comes to executive coaching, sharing is an intrinsic part of the process, from both the coach and client's perspectives. As a coach, what can I share that will best help my client? How will listening and relating to my client's thoughts, emotions and experiences help them to advance their agenda and achieve their objectives? It's not about me or my coaching skills, but how I choose to 'show up' in a way that resonates and helps my clients. From a client's perspective, they share elements of their life, goals, ideas, worries and thoughts, all of which are important to them. They choose how they 'show up' for the coaching session. Many clients use coaching as a means to transform their own behaviours in order to benefit their business and improve as leaders. Just like the musicians, they need to go from being functional experts to storytellers.

So I'll leave you with few questions to ponder:

- What do I want to share with the world?

- What is my unique story?

- If it's not about me, who is it about? Just like the musicians – how might I transform my expertise into a unique story that resonates with my audience?

- How do I want to 'show up' – mentally, physically, emotionally?

- How might sharing something different or new benefit my 'audience'?

- What can I share that I haven't shared before?

Creativity through climate control

Nicholas Wai

It's always refreshing to listen to Sir Ken Robinson talk about education, as he has such a funny and accessible approach that helps you to really understand the issues. No wonder his first TED talk is one of the most popular amongst the thousands available online, and I am quite sure his latest TED talk[26] about creativity and education will attract a similar following. In this talk – 'How to escape Education's Death Valley', Robinson explains why the education systems in many countries are not working, with high dropout rates and low effectiveness. He reasons that part of the problem is the command and control system that is practiced by many of the developed economies, where a central authority dictates what and sometimes even how to teach, without regard for the personalities and individual talents of the students.

Instead, he argues that schools should adopt a 'climate-control' system to create an environment in which children can use their natural curiosity and talent to learn and grow. He uses Death Valley in California as a metaphor: it has always been barren, as it almost never rains there. But one year there was heavy rainfall, and Death Valley came to life as flowers and plants flourished. People realised that the valley was actually not without vegetation, it were just dormant. His conclusion is that in the right conditions, people will be free to use their talents to create and thrive, instead of having them lie dormant. So the challenge for us is to understand our talents and the environment in which they will come alive and thrive.

---

26 [website] *Ken Robinson: How to escape education's death... | TED.com*

But how do we create the right environment? For this we can turn to another very popular TED speaker, Ben Zander[27]. Ben is the conductor of the Boston Philharmonic Orchestra, and with his wife Ros he wrote a book called *The Art of Possibility.* It describes how he turned his orchestra into a group where everyone is a leader, everyone is fully committed and makes contributions, and everyone thoroughly enjoys what they do. Ben first came to the conclusion that he needed to create the right environment for his orchestra to come alive when he realised that the conductor was the only person in the orchestra that does not make a sound, and has to rely on every other member of the orchestra to do their very best work together to create beautiful music.

In the book, he describes the 12 points that he believes are important in this quest, which are equally applicable to other environments. I still remember the impression it made when I first read the book – especially Rule No. 6: don't take yourself so seriously! How often do we get angry or all worked up because we don't get our way? More often than not, if we can calm down and look at the situation from different angles, we can find other possibilities and realise that our anger is trapping us in a box we create for ourselves. This simple rule helps me release the pressure I put on myself and creates space for creativity to happen. I have to remind myself of it once in a while, when things got too tense or if I am being too self-centred, and it works every time.

---

27 [website] *Benjamin Zander - Music and passion | TED.com*

CHAPTER 6

WHAT NOW?
CREATING THE FUTURE

Kilometer 9,000:
looking back and looking ahead

Charlotte Rydlund

I **wrote** a series during my career transition to force myself to reflect. And indeed, I say *force*, because the CANADIVE expedition was so full of action that it was easy to let the much-needed quality reflection time to slide another day, another week, another month. Reflection was vital because there were only three weeks to go before the official end of the expedition, which meant the question of *what's next?* was ringing in my ears, and becoming louder by the day.

So how did I approach this question?

Firstly, the action I refer to in the expedition was not only about being constantly on the move. I was *doing* things: scuba diving, budgeting and keeping track of our finances, marketing strategy and execution, ongoing project management, PR and media relations, writing, monitoring online activities, managing partner relations, negotiating with local shops, using coaching skills, and of course, ongoing teamwork and communication with my teammate (and husband). Besides the diving, that list of skills could easily be a corporate job description (or a part of several job descriptions). This made me realize that although I was far from the corporate life (at least in geographical distance!), my skills were very transferable to completely different settings.

Secondly, transition is not static. One of the reasons for the CANADIVE Expedition was to transition to a new career and way of life, while channelling my skills and one of my passions into something that enabled action, awareness and involvement around marine debris. The expedition had a finite lifespan of four months that we had set for ourselves, but I realized that my career transition would not be over at the end of the four months-and neither would the mantra that we had created through the expedition ('Make every dive a clean-up dive').

A few points that came together as an important *'A-ha!'* moment that made the *'What's next?'* question even more exciting was my realization and confirmation that my skills were indeed transferable (tried and tested in action), as well as a new perspective that my own transition was not really over when the expedition was over.

I leave you with these few tips when looking towards the future:

- **Keep your reflection time.** Do not put it off. Make a date with yourself, or get someone to hold you accountable – whatever way works for you. Writing this monthly series was my way to keep myself accountable and reflect consistently, and so far it's working.

- **Be creative in how you apply your skills.** With an open mind, resourcefulness and a little distance from routine, your skills become less specific to a certain job or function, and can become flexible, adaptable and useful in completely different situations.

- **Embrace the realisation that transition is not static but fluid.** Transition is an ongoing process. The only deadlines are the ones you set for yourself. We had set four months for the CANADIVE Expedition, which made financial sense for us and was a good checkpoint before settling down. But until that point, I had seen the duration of the expedition and my career transition as being one and the same. After reflecting, I intentionally separated the end of the expedition from my 'completed' career transition. It was just the beginning.

Diversity has always been here: how do we communicate it better?

Yvonne Thackray

I **started** by asking myself how being cross-cultural has impacted me personally. I am a British-born Chinese who grew up in a small conservative town, and my entrepreneurial parents owned a family business in the east of England. I studied at the local grammar school and completed my degree in civil engineering in one of the top departments in the UK (and the USA as part of an exchange program). I worked in a number of roles as an engineer in the UK and in Hong Kong. I then worked as a consultant on projects ranging from executive coaching and organising and facilitating workshops for a range of non-profit, quasi-governmental and for-profit organisations in Asia. And now I am expanding my knowledge into social and cultural anthropology – bringing this together with coaching. Besides being a life-long learner, the only answer I could come up with is I have always lived and worked in diverse environments: it's a part of my day-to-day life.

I don't remember a time when I haven't interacted, studied and worked in a dynamic and cross-cultural environment. To live in a homogenous monocultural environment – I can't imagine what *that* would be like! We connect with each other on common core interests like education, profession, social activities, religions, etc. and our differences are often exacerbated by the stereotypes and unconscious biases we have based on gender, social class, ethnicity, sexuality etc. Sometimes it's easy to blame those differences when things don't go our way, especially when we have a fixed mind-set or are too focused on something specific. It becomes harder to see the other person's points of view and respect how they might have come to their position when we no longer have the capacity to empathise with them.

Conflict can quickly manifest when we stop listening to and being empathetic towards the other party, and begin to objectify them. We may either start to blame the person rather than listen to their reasoning or rationalise his/her behaviour as being based on cultural upbringing, gender, ethnicity, social class, religious beliefs etc. It can be extremely easy to generalise rather than search for the truth, which can often be found below the surface. I am not suggesting that when there is a conflict you should go along and agree with the other person – I believe that we can agree to disagree, but we should come from a place where we at least agree on the common facts even if our interpretations differ. Those interpretations will be the result of our intellectual capacity, enculturation, values and beliefs, and we need to be able to respect how an individual comes to their own opinion.

Ultimately, who we are as an individual is the result of our personality, culture and experiences. However, when a situation arises in which we notice we are absent-mindedly rationalizing the speaker's point of view and/or generalizing their behaviour, we should take a moment to check those assumptions we arrived at so easily. I recommend 3 simple tips that we probably learned when we were growing up, that are also key tenets of coaching:

- **Listen:** Pay attention and listen to what's been said.

- **Observe:** Observe how you are responding to what's been said, and physically observe how the person is speaking to you.

- **Ask:** Ask questions to clarify when you notice you might have a different interpretation of what's been said; focus on the facts of the conversation rather than engaging with the emotional aspect unless it's appropriate.

I believe we do this most of the time without realizing it, but when we are under pressure, all that can go out the window. That is when we need to step back and quickly run through these tips.

Chemistry + intuition = first impressions

Charlotte Rydlund

I**can recall** several occasions when I met someone for the first time and just got the feeling that the chemistry wasn't there. No matter how much effort I put into conversation, it felt like pulling teeth, and for someone who is extroverted and likes people, I found it very frustrating that I couldn't seem to find common ground with them. Looking back at those instances, I realize that my intuition (or gut feeling) was right from the start, even if the conversation went for a little while, or if I met them again.

I've had other first-time encounters where it was exactly the opposite. I can remember several occasions where we didn't even have to speak to each other, I just had a sense that we were going to get along. Whether it's body language or tone of voice, these are unspoken factors that contribute to overall chemistry. And in these cases, the chemistry just worked. Conversation was easy, and body language was relaxed. I've been lucky to have several of these encounters, and the people I've met through them have become great business partners or life-long friends.

I can't say if I took note of all of the cues in those encounters right away. Most of the time I have only confirmed my intuition after the fact (for better or worse). But overall, whether I note it at the time or afterwards, my gut feeling has usually been fairly accurate, whether it was based on cues I noted from body language (like a hand shake or eye contact) or tone of voice, for example, in combination with the tone of the conversation.

So what is it about first impressions and following your gut that is so important? I have heard several times that non-verbal communication (body language, facial expressions, and so on) make up a large percentage of what is communicated to others, and according to the nonverbalgroup.com, non-verbal communication makes up 75-90% of what we say. This leaves very little space to transmit a message in words.

Could we say that the most important part of a first encounter is a combination of chemistry and gut feeling (intuition)? Does this mean that building trust from a first impression happens before we even speak? And if first impressions are mostly non-verbal, then how much can we actually impact the situation by talking? Does it really all come down to chemistry and the intuitive gut feeling when determining how good or bad a relationship is going to be?

First impressions are the result of combining chemistry and intuition, and I feel that chemistry is part of being human, and that intuition – that gut feeling – is something that can be practiced and honed. I recently read an article about 10 thing that intuitive people do differently[28] – and this inspired me to work more on my intuition. What inspires you to work on your intuition?

A few questions to think about when training your intuition:

- When was a time when you experienced a 'spot-on' gut feeling?
- What did you do with that gut feeling?
- How much of what you recall was verbal and non-verbal?
- What did you learn from that experience?
- What might you try differently next time?

---

28 [website] *10 Things Highly Intuitive People Do Differently | HuffingtonPost.com*

Keep calm and count my blessings

Nicholas Wai

One time I had an issue with a company I was thinking of joining as a contractor, because it messed up my schedule and failed to honour an understanding which I thought was mutual – and I allowed this to negatively impact other areas of my life. The anger I felt infected my day and I'm ashamed to say that I channelled it by unfairly taking it out on others. I didn't like this about myself, but I let it drag on. If I were my coach, I would ask myself: 'Anger stems from thinking that you have been treated unfairly. How have you been treated unfairly?' The answer to that would then lead to a second set of questions: 'So what exactly did they do or not do that lead to this unfairness?' 'Are they aware of it?' 'If you can do anything, what would you do to right the situation?'

I started a coaching book club here in Hong Kong, and at our first meeting we discussed *Flourish* by Martin Seligman, the person whom we owe the discipline of positive psychology to. There are many nuggets of wisdom in the book, but one that has proven particularly useful is 'count your blessings'. I had allowed a minor frustration to become magnified out of all proportion, and in realising this, I can now take responsibility for allowing this by not directly clearing up the matter with the party concerned. I could use 'count your blessings' to put things into perspective by taking stock of what happened in our lives during the year – especially those good things that have come our way.

Looking back, I was very grateful that my adventure into coaching and facilitating has been very fruitful. I not only gained a lot of experience by facilitating workshops, meetings and working with many new clients, but also took the next step to create workshops on topics which I am passionate about. I got to give back to the community by organising coaching outreach sessions and start a book club with like-minded coaches and coachees who were into discussing the books I was interested in reading and sharing. I also built up a professional reputation that led other training and coaching companies to approach me about working on projects with them. I couldn't have planned it better, and I am really proud of what I have achieved thus far.

Did 'counting my blessings' help me turn my mood around in thinking about that incident? I think it definitely did. After counting my blessings, I became more able to put things into perspective and take on the issue with more positivity and confidence, rather than let it control me. I also found the positive effect of counting and cataloguing my blessings, was like having a store of goodwill that I could revisit whenever I needed. Nothing beats a first-hand learning experience!

Myers-Briggs type indicator and change

Charlotte Rydlund

It **is indeed** important to count our blessings. Change however is inevitable. How does change affect us and how do we react to it? Here is an overview of how we may be inclined to react while experiencing change, using the Myers-Briggs Type Indicator.

m
y
e
r
s
-
b
r
i
g
g
s
•
c
h
a
n
g
e
•

Myers-Briggs and change

MBTI

The MBTI (Myers-Briggs Type Indicator) is based on psychologist Carl Jung's theory on Psychological types, and further expanded by mother-daughter team Myers-Briggs.

The underlying idea is that each of us has a certain preference as to where we get our energy from, what type of information we seek and how we interpret it, the process by which we make decisions, and how we interact with the outside world.

Change

Change is inevitable, and something we can choose to embrace, avoid, repel, influence, or just go along with the flow.

We all know more or less how we might respond to change in different situations (and maybe we wish we might have responded differently?)

Whether your reaction is instinctive, emotional or completely rational – we all have a response.

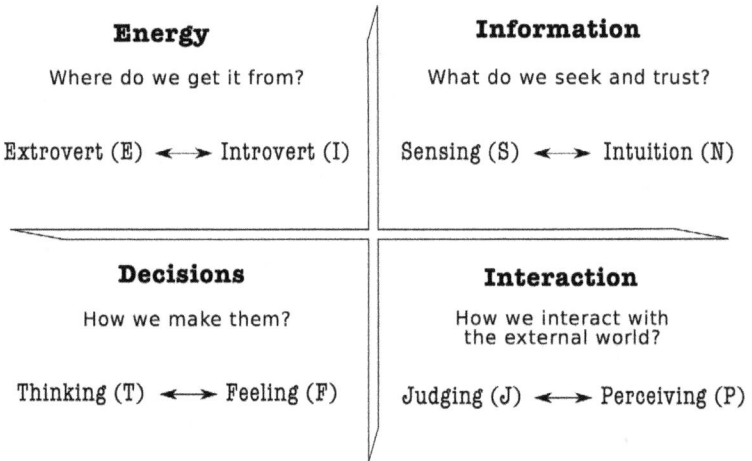

Energy

Where do we get it from?

Extrovert (E) ←→ Introvert (I)

Information

What do we seek and trust?

Sensing (S) ←→ Intuition (N)

Decisions

How we make them?

Thinking (T) ←→ Feeling (F)

Interaction

How we interact with the external world?

Judging (J) ←→ Perceiving (P)

What happens if we mix our own MBTI preferences into a situation of change?

MBTI + Change = NEEDS

'I need time to talk, involvement, lots of communication, get attention, action.'
EXTROVERT

'I need overall rationale, general plan, picture of the future, options, change to participate in designing the future.'
INTUITION

'I need logic and reason, clarity on decision making and goals, competent leadership, fairness/ equitability in changes.'
THINKING

'I need real data, specifics and details, realistic, clear roles & responsibilities.'
SENSING

'I need time to reflect, think and assimilate information, be asked their opinion, through-out written communication.'
INTROVERSION

'I need an open-ended plan, general parameters, flexibility, room to adjust.'
PERCEIVING

'I need to know the impact of change on people, inclusion, values, leadership that cares, appreciation and support.'
FEELING

'I need clear priorities, action plan and timeframe, defined outcome and goals, completion, no surprises.'
JUDGING

m y e r s - b r i g g s • c h a n g e

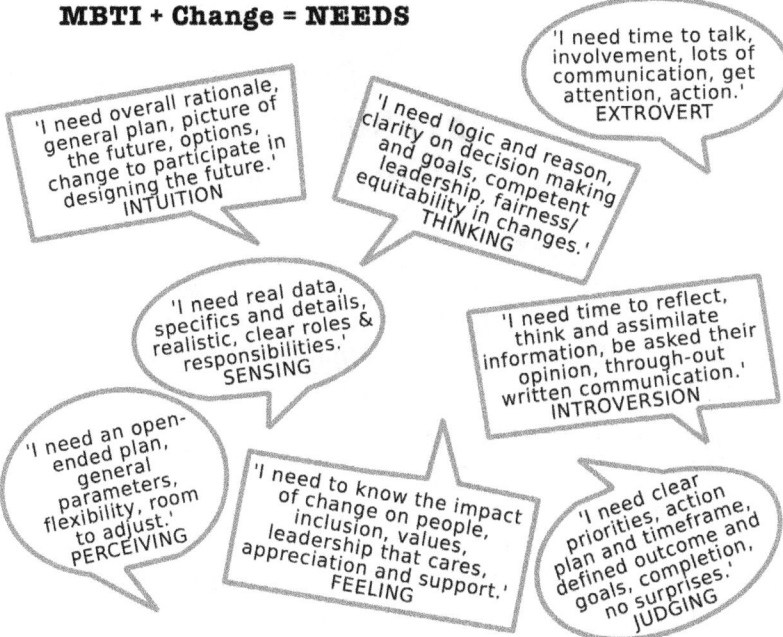

Key take-outs

1. The MBTI is a versatile tool for managing change for individuals, coaches, leaders and organisations.

2. Stay focused on the client's agenda – irrespective of how much we think we know as coaches, focus on the client's agenda in a learner mindset, and coach the individual, not just their MBTI profile. Avoid making assumptions about the individual on the basis of their MBTI preferences.

3. Build trust with your client by adapting your language to better match your client's MBTI preferences and mirror the language they use in their coaching conversation.
(How many ways are there to ask the same question?)

Am I influencing culture,
or is culture influencing me?

Yvonne Thackray

'Each man must look to himself to teach him the meaning of life. It is not something discovered; it is something moulded.'

– Antoine de Saint-Exupery [29]

Is being a part of something more important than having respect, or are we looking to both belong and be respected? Culture is one of those words that I believe will evolve over time because it embraces many broad concepts. I define culture here as 'the ideas, customs, and social behaviour of a particular people or society' (Oxforddictionaries.com). In our daily life we interact with many cultures, and we constantly switch between them – sometimes with ease and sometimes with difficulty, depending on where we believe we belong. From when we are born, we are taught the values and norms of our birth culture by our family – knowledge which is vital for functioning within that cultural context. Then, we learn to socialize with others, learning new skills and languages to interact with other individuals. This process of enculturation and socialization is a continuous process that is both transient and dynamic, and it helps us adapt to the different cultures we interact with on a daily basis.

As human beings, we are social creatures and so we have an innate desire to 'belong' within a group. The question then becomes, how much of ourselves do we disclose in order to

---

29 [website] *Antoine de Saint-Exupery Quotes | BrainyQuote*

belong, and which aspects of our identity do we choose to hide because we fear being discriminated against by others? A fear of discrimination may be translated as 'losing respect' in the eyes of the other whose opinion you may or may not value because you are now being treated unfairly.

> *'Lack of respect, though less aggressive than an outright insult, can take an equally wounding form. No insult is another person, but neither is recognition extended; he or she is not – as a full human being whose presence matters.'[30]*

– Richard Sennet

And so, when we ask the question, 'Who am I?', the answer may not be as straightforward as we first thought because we could be the sum of all the cultures we belong to, either by choice or circumstance. How many groups do you belong to, and can you articulate what they are? Even if the balance between belonging and respect is not optimal, where do you stand within these cultures?

- Fully belonging and fully respected

- Fully belonging and somewhat respected

- Fully respected and somewhat belonging

- Do not belong and not respected

Being able to discover which cultures fulfil you more will also help you to deepen your understanding of what's valuable to you as an individual. Take the time to reflect and consider which cultures have helped you become the person you are today?

---

30 Sennet, R. (2003). *Respect: The Formation of Character in an Age of Inequality.*

CHAPTER 7

THE VALUE OF COACHING

Lending an ear... even if you were the Prime Minister

Nicholas Wai

I **do** miss living in London sometimes... walking in the parks when the weather is nice (and dancing in the rain when it is not), strolling around the world-famous museums and galleries whenever you like (even for 10 minutes, as they are free), listening to world-class thinkers and speakers talk about their research at the Royal Society of Art, and taking classes in anything that take your fancy (from furniture design to bowmaking). Of course, there is also the option of going to concerts and plays any time you want. But luckily, with technology these days, one can watch a performance from the National Theatre at a local cinema in your own city, which I took advantage of to see Peter Morgan's *The Audience,* with Helen Mirren playing Queen Elizabeth II.

Every Tuesday, the Queen and her Prime Minister meet for half an hour. There is no-one else there, and no minutes are taken. In theory, they could talk about anything and with no official record, no one would ever know what was said. Intrigued by these mysterious meeting, the playwright imagined what might have actually happened at these meetings. With a cast of 'ready-made' strong characters (the Queen has had 12 different Prime Ministers so far, from Winston Churchill when she was 25 to David Cameron, who is younger than her youngest child), Morgan created a play that is both dramatic and funny, with clever dialogue (and flawless acting to match).

What I found fascinating was that the Prime Ministers featured, who are among the most powerful people in the country, could not have talked freely with anyone else without worrying that what they said might be used against them. The Queen, who occupies a privileged position, could be trusted to keep absolute confidence; some PMs appreciated the opportunity to share their most intimate insecurities and worries with their sovereign, who had grown in strength and confidence over time but had also developed understanding and compassion. In one great scene in which the Queen hears about the passing of Margaret Thatcher, whom she reportedly did not much warm to, she remarked that they were only 6 months apart in age in a tone that revealed her sense of loss and respect, which we had previously glimpsed when they debated fiercely about sanctions against South Africa in an earlier scene.

In coaching, we often work with top executives who are in similar situations, where they cannot talk freely with people in their own organisations or reveal their worries and insecurities because of their positions, but still need an outlet. In coaches, they look for trusted allies with whom they can feel free to disclose their inner-thinking, and discuss different ways of handling them. As coaches we are not there to judge or counsel (although suggestions are sometimes requested for consideration), but to listen with a level of understanding and compassion that will make them feel safe and confident enough to let down their guard and be vulnerable, so self-examination and growth can occur. It might be a passive role, but it is nevertheless important to hold up a mirror and be someone whom they can bounce ideas off. We can all benefit from a trusted ally like the Queen – she provided a vital outlet for the Prime Ministers of the UK as a trusted listener to whom they could reveal their innermost concerns.

To be coached, or not to be coached, that is the question

Yvonne Thackray

Coaching is not a new phenomenon, but it is an effective tool that fits into our culture, which operates in a 'just-in-time' mode. Living and working in a just-in-time culture has reduced our ability to focus on the future, as we spend a significant proportion of our time reacting to and making decisions about the challenges affecting us right now. Coaching works because we crave the space to think about our future, and that is what makes it unique. Taking time to meet with a coach is about regaining control of one's time and deciding how it should be used. Being in a session with a coach provides that opportunity to explore the stresses of the challenge at hand, and how to handle the future now. Through the sessions insights are derived that can turn into positive actions, because the private time allows one to explore both the big picture and the detail from different perspectives. And by the time a session is complete, a sense of peace, clarity, focus or intention of how to move forward has been achieved on one's own terms.

It begins with having meaningful goals because this stirs the fire within us to keep at the challenge we are committed to. It grounds us because energy is generated between our goal and motivation. Goals can be driven by an internal need, an external pressure, or a combination of both. Sustained motivation comes from harmony between our rational and emotional selves. When they both come together in a productive environment, it ignites a spark within that motivates us to make a change and stay on course. At various points in the coaching process, different coaching positions are needed. The coach needs to judge the situation from one moment to the next, and decide what approach is required to support the client in moving forward: making the coaching experience more fun and enjoyable is a bonus.

- **Reflective coaching:** this might be used to uncover what it is that's holding you back from achieving your goal and find compassionate ways to move forward, either as baby steps or with one giant leap. Or it's good for open-mindedly reviewing your purpose and exploring ways to fulfil it even more. The coach provides a safe space to allow you to reflect and fearlessly verbalise the challenges you are setting yourself.

- **Strategic coaching:** this is used to work out the strategies necessary to achieve your goal, whether it's thinking of alternative ways of completing an action, identifying collaborators or those whom you can delegate work to, or deciding what new techniques you either require or must build on. Bouncing strategies back and forth with a peer coach will help you to find the most appropriate and proactive pathway to achieving success.

- **Accountability coaching:** this is used when you have already formulated your strategy and you want a coach to compassionately hold you accountable to it, and provide a safe space in which to review what went well and what went badly when taking action. Having space to openly reflect with the support of a coach will improve your awareness and decision-making capacities in a neutral place.

These are just some of the ways in which coaching can support you whenever you decide that you need extra support on your journey. To be coached, or not to be coached, that is the question; it serves those who believe that:

'The future belongs to those who believe in the beauty of their dreams'

– Eleanor Roosevelt [31]

31 [website] *Eleanor Roosevelt Quotes | BrainyQuote*

Would a coach benefit from having a coach? You bet!

Nicholas Wai

Why would a coach want to work with a mentor coach (a coach's coach who would support and help a fellow coach to reflect and progress)?, you might ask. And my response would be that a mentor coach is one of the most valuable resources a coach can have. I must admit that I only started mentor-coaching because it is one of the accreditation requirements for the International Coach Federation (ICF), one of the professional bodies that aims to uphold the standards and professionalism of coaches around the world. Nevertheless, after experiencing the joys and benefits of mentor-coaching in both a group and one-on-one setting, I would say that having a mentor coach is a necessity for any coach who would like to stay clear-headed while at the same time continuously improving his or her skills and expertise in supporting their clients.

A coaching relationship has often been described as a partnership in learning and self-improvement; a mentor-coaching relationship is a valuable resource that helps me to make sure that I am playing my best game and never stop improving as a coach. So how is a mentor-coaching session structured? In a group mentor-coaching session, we would either perform a live coaching session for about 15 minutes with two of the participants, or listen to a recorded session by one of the participating coaches (with the prior approval of the client). Then, led by a more experienced and senior mentor coach, we would provide feedback on how the coach performed with reference to the core coaching competencies[32] stipulated by the ICF. (This was done in confidence and with the permission of the coaches being critiqued.) In a one-on-one session, on the other hand, the mentor coach and I would listen to a recorded coaching session and then carefully go through and offer feedback on each of the core competencies to help facilitate self-reflection and growth.

So what have I got out of my 10 hours of mentor-coaching, and why would I say that mentor-coaching is a necessity for any coach even outside of the credentialing process?

- A clear and objective perspective on my coaching skills from a more experienced colleague.

- A professional relationship with someone I trust and value, who I can ask questions or bounce ideas off.

- Having someone to hold me accountable for change and growth.

- Group mentor-coaching provides a unique opportunity to learn from and discuss professional matters with a diverse group of colleagues.

- It is also a great opportunity and honour to support and give back to the coaching community by helping to raise and maintain standards and to share knowledge.

---

32 [website] *Core Competencies - Individual Credentialing | ICF*

Being present for reflection

Naomi Dishington

The word 'reflection' derives from the Latin word *reflexio*, and one of its definitions is 'the act of bending back.' By periodically engaging in focused reflection, we discover that 'bending back' actually helps to propel us forward. Good coaching will facilitate this process of analytical self-discovery.

So, how does coaching, which is focused mainly on the *future*, use reflection, which is largely focused on the *past*, to help achieve presence, which is about right *now*?

The goal of coaching is to facilitate growth and change in an individual or group. If we think of reflection as 'the process by which experience is turned into knowledge'[33], it is clear that reflection lies at the centre of the learning process. In 'bending back' to consider a past event or pattern, we learn to analyse our thoughts, feelings and actions. Coaching provides some structure around this process and helps us make transformative adjustments based on our reflections. For example:

- What worked well?
- What didn't go as planned?
- How did it feel?
- What did you learn?
- What would you like to do differently in the future?

33 Gilbert, W. & Trudel, P. (2001). 'Learning to coach through experience: Reflection in model youth sport coaches'.

You may be wondering why you need a coach to benefit from reflection. If you are like most people, you might feel some anxiety about slowing down long enough to reflect. After all, modern society values action, decisiveness, and movement. Who has time to unplug, sit and reflect? Many of us do not prioritize slowing down, turning inward, or being present. We might also be unsure about where to focus our attention during reflection. Perhaps we don't know which questions to ask ourselves? Working with a coach can help you overcome these barriers, because he/she brings a framework that guides the process.

One part of that framework is the use of questions that guide the reflective process. Depending on the client's stated goals[34], these might include:

- **Clarifying questions** – the coach guides the client to recall significant events and describe his/her feelings, actions or thoughts.

- **Consequential questions** – the coach helps the client determine the cause and effect of certain actions or beliefs.

- **Linking questions** – the coach prompts an examination of possible connections between the circumstances around a situation and the personal beliefs, values, and goals of a client.

When asking questions of this nature, a coach must keep in mind the professional boundary between coaching and therapy, but assuming he/she is working with mentally healthy adults, these questions are appropriate in a coaching setting.

In addition to asking insightful questions, coaches might also suggest reflective journaling assignments. One useful journaling template, suggested by D. Francis[35], includes the following prompts:

- **Describe:** what did I do? (without judgement)

- **Inform:** what does this mean?
  (patterns or beliefs behind behaviour)

---

34 Barnett, B. (1995). 'Developing Reflection and Expertise: Can Mentors Make the Difference?'
35 Francis, D. (1995). 'The Reflective Journal: A Window to Preserve Teachers' Practical Knowledge'.

- **Confront:** how did I come to be this way? (examining social/cultural aspects)

- **Reconstruct:** how could I do this differently? (alternative views)

A third technique that a coach can use is to literally reflect back the words, thoughts, and feelings they hear. A coach might say, 'You sound hesitant about that,' or 'I hear some anger in your voice,' or 'Your eyes lit up when you said that.' Having a coach reflect back at you is crucial to developing your own reflective practice. And being given the silent space to process all of it is priceless.

As you continue to cultivate your ability to be present, I hope you will consider developing your reflective skills as well. The two competencies really are mutually beneficial.

> *'Follow effective action with quiet reflection. From the quiet reflection will come even more effective action.'*

> **– Peter F. Drucker**[36]

36 [website] *Peter Drucker Quotes | BrainyQuote*

Executive presence: the key to the executive suite!

Yvonne Thackray

Executive presence is about building one's character within an organisation. This takes time, because character has to do with the way we perceive ourselves whilst consistently aligning one's actions to fit one's behaviours and expectations, as well as being something that's valued by others. And executive presence has also been identified as an area for development for many leaders, executives, managers, human resources and talent management professionals within organisations. But what is executive presence? That is what I aim to demystify here.

Executive Presence: the key to the executive suite

What is it? 'A person with executive or leadership presence is someone, who by virtue of the effect he or she has on an audience, exerts influence beyond that conferred by formal authority.' – **Levitt (2013)**

Presence vs. Leadership

Effective leadership is about causing people to act. Effective presence is about causing people to listen.

Why Executive Presence?

According to a survey carried out in 2012 by the Center for Talent Innovation, 268 senior US executives reported that 'being perceived as leadership material is essential to being promoted into leadership positions,' and executive presence accounts for, on average, 25% of what it takes to get promoted.

The Ridler Report 2013 on 'Trends in the Use of Executive Coaching' reported that amongst the 145 respondents, of which 77% are based in the UK, over 60% used coaching to support transitions arising from internal promotion.

What are the key characteristics that drive presence?

A recent report, 'Executive Presence: Influence beyond authority", completed in March 2013 by Dr Gavin R. Dagley in association with the Australian Human Resources Institute, indicated that 'presence changes over time' and derived 10 characteristics, split into 2 categories, that drive presence and influence over time.

Characteristics that drive early impressions	**Characteristics that determine presence in long term relationships**
– Status and reputation – Physical characteristics i.e. poise and appearance – Demeanour i.e. confidence and gravitas – Communication skills including quality of speech, active listening and assertiveness – Interpersonal skills to quickly engage and connect	– Interpersonal behaviour patterns relating to quality of interactions & relationships over time – Values-in-action – Intellect and expertise – Outcome delivery ability includes leadership responsibility associated with driving results – Power use: leader's role vs. how power is used by leaders

What next? If you believe that executive presence is your missing piece... invest in yourself!

Independently, or with an independent and impartial partner, take the time to realistically assess your presence as observed by others and yourself in different situations.

Identify which characteristics are working well and which might be holding you back from progressing within the organisation. Check this list with a few people whose judgement you trust.

Choose the characteristics of presence you want to improve at work, and focus on improvement by attending training, reading on the subject, finding a mentor, or partnering with a coach. Executive Presence is important in your current job and the key to your next role!

e x e c u t i v e • p r e s e n c e •

High-performance teams go beyond expertise

Charlotte Rydlund

Think about the best team you were ever a part of. Was it an existing team or a newly formed one? What was it like joining the team? How did you feel when you joined the team, and how did the team dynamic evolve? What's unique about this one team?

I believe that most teams go through Tuckman's stages of group development: Forming, Storming, Norming and Performing. This was a theory shared by Bruce Tuckman[37] in the 1960s, and has formed the basis for many group theories since then. The stages of group development chart how group behaviours change and develop as the members of a group get acquainted with each other. It describes the process by which everyone finds their place in the group (forming, storming, norming), and how each member adds unique value to the group while working towards a common goal (performing).

Now, with this group development theory in mind, let's go through the simple exercise that we started at the beginning of this essay and delve a little deeper. Think of your best team. How did your team go through the group development stages? Did your team move through all of the stages and deliver high performance? What did you learn? What happened when a new team member joined, or someone in the team left? Did the group go through another cycle of group development?

---

37 [website] *Tuckman's stages of group development |*
Wikipedia, the free encyclopedia

Teams are brought together because each individual brings a certain expertise, and through the team, that individual expertise is integrated with that of the others to achieve a common goal. Ideally, in every team the 'whole is greater than the sum of their parts'[38]. Today, more often than not, teams are not located in the same geographical location; instead, they work as virtual teams spread across the globe. I have worked on projects with people in different parts of the world, some of whom I have never met. Wherever we are located – be it in Europe, North America, Asia or elsewhere, there is a feeling of a team working towards a shared goal.

What is it, then, that enables a team to progress through the stages – be it virtually or face-to-face? I would argue that this is not purely based on functional expertise. An individual is normally selected and brought into a team because of their unique skills. However, one cannot ignore that each individual team member is more than an expert in a field – they are also a person. And this is what can make or break a team, influencing whether it will evolve through all the group development stages and achieve its goals. Individual needs, wants, motivations and communication styles all contribute to a chemistry which influences the interaction and performance of the team as a whole.

Here are the key behaviours that are essential for creating the chemistry for a high- performing team:

- **Mutual trust and respect:** these are underlying factors that come before everything else. Trust and respect are intrinsic to any strong relationship, and even more so within a team because there are many 'moving parts'. In my experience, trust and mutual respect in high-performing teams are established from the start (as opposed to other situations where it is expected to be earned). How do you display trust and respect in your team? What comes first in your team – trust or respect? What type of framework or process might your team use to facilitate and nurture mutual trust and respect?

---

38 Famously quoted by Aristotle. [website] *Aristotle Quotes* | *BrainyQuote*

- **Appreciation of strengths:** each team member has key strengths, be it functional, behavioural, or a combination of both, and appreciating an individual's different strengths is key. While some strengths might overlap with those of other team members, others might be unique to an individual member. Getting this balance right is the key to a strong team. Teams are often brought together for functional expertise over anything else, but the teams I have been a part of that also know how to understand (and leverage) each other's behavioural strengths to perform better. What are your team's key strengths, and how might you leverage them more effectively?

- **Learner mindset:** being curious and open to learning transforms the dynamic in a team immediately. When there are questions, challenges, and discussions within a team with a shared learner mindset, it leads to innovative ideas and actions that further fuel the team's momentum. It nurtures a shared motivation to make constant improvements, all geared towards reaching the team's goal(s). What have you learned from your team? What is your team's approach to capturing those learning-rich moments?

- **Open Communication:** Combined with the other behaviours above, open communication makes supporting and challenging ideas an inclusive and positive means of moving towards a common goal. It aids the evolution towards higher performance and beyond, not only for individuals, but the team as a whole. Open communication is vital, especially when working in virtual teams where the written or spoken word is used to build a rapport within a team (compared to factors like body language, which are more important in face-to-face situations). Very often, embracing and mastering different communication styles is a key part of the group development process. What methods has your team used to maintain open communication channels between its members?

Afterword & acknowledgements

Before we begin our afterword and acknowledgements, we think you would be interested to find out how Charlotte's journey came to an end. Wait no longer! Charlotte shares her final reflections:

When I set out to do the CANADIVE Expedition, I had several plans and objectives: 1) do something good while doing something we love in our new country of residence 2) drive 10,000 km across Canada and mobilize local communities to clean up 99 sites while scuba diving, 3) take this time to transition from my corporate world and life to an independent be-my-own-boss life and to document my journey.

So how did these pan out?

Firstly, we did do something good while doing something we loved. We cleaned up 99 sites with local communities and divers, met some inspiring people, and got some amazing media coverage from local newspapers and local and regional radio as well as regional TV. We created awareness beyond the diving community about a global issue that is important to us in a way that was positive, action-driven and locally relevant.

Secondly, we did drive 10,000 km, and then another 10,000 km, and then 3,000 km more. It's more than double what was originally planned, and more than 50% of the Earth's circumference. Quite a journey, especially when living in a tent!

Thirdly, transitioning from the corporate to the independent life definitely happened. I am thankful to have taken the opportunity to document my journey and to have had this expedition as a full-time activity while making the transition. But the end date of the expedition was not the end date of my transition. I realized that my transition was far from over because transition and change is fluid. But, the transition continued to take me forward towards where I wanted to go. I definitely did not take the most direct route, but it was definitely a life-changing adventure.

Looking back at my transition, here are the lessons learned:

- **Be prepared for changes in your journey – we planned for 10,000 km and it took us 23,000 km instead.** *We didn't always take the fastest or most direct route, but instead we took the route that was the most fulfilling, meaningful, and right for us. We did arrive at our destination and our goal, but not necessarily in the way we had planned. As long as you keep your goal in the forefront of your mind, you will reach it, irrespective of the route you take.*

- **Transition is a journey, and one to document, both for your own growth, and also as a little ego-boost.** *Having a checkpoint – for me, it was writing the monthly account of my transition – was helpful to reflect on what was happening in real-time, and to re-direct any misgivings, emotions or set-backs towards moving forward and achieving my goals. By having a checkpoint, you can actually look back and see how much you have accomplished and how much you have learned (and you can feel a little bit proud too!)*

- **Don't take yourself too seriously – transition is an attitude and an adventure.** *And I speak for myself – I can often be very serious – but seriousness can dampen the fun and also the potential opportunities and experiences that can come with a transition. Not everyone has the chance (or takes the chance) to make a change. Seek the chance, and take the chance to make a change – you might even enjoy it!*

Much Ado About Coaching came into being through opportunity and synchronicity. All the contributing authors started their journey by writing blogs, sharing their stories and describing the changes that influenced their life journey over the course of 18 months. Simply by writing snippets about what was important to us, we generated many stories, essays and infographics and a couple of us began to ask what could we do next. Partially inspired by American blogger, entrepreneur, weightlifter and travel photographer James Clear's post on goals and systems (Oct 28, 2013), we saw an opportunity to push our envelopes and do something we would not have conceived trying on our own – writing a book!

We were inspired by our own stories and the feedback we received from our readers. We began asking ourselves questions about what coaching really meant for us. Whilst reviewing our essays, we realised that our key strength was offering different opinions and viewpoints to spark conversations (which can last a long time in our meetings) that sometimes became antagonistic but always returned to humour and compassion. This interplay reminded us of one of our favourite plays, which in turn inspired the title of this book. How grateful we are to Shakespeare's *Much Ado About Nothing!*

We also wanted to create a precedent for working together. It's very easy in our line of work to freely give away one's work and gratefully accept the recognition that comes from being mentioned in someone else's book as a reward (see 'A Note of Contractual Agreement'). So we took an alternative approach, and wrote into our legal agreement that all authors contributing to *Much Ado About Coaching* retained ownership of their own material whilst allowing the project owners to publish their work in the volume you now hold. If the book sells well, we hope to fairly share some of the financial equity with the contributors. We want to change the *status quo* of how coaches work together, and inspire you to do the same!

When it comes to pulling this book together, we not only have to thank all the authors (Yvonne Thackray, Charlotte Rydlund, Nicholas Wai, Naomi Dishington and Wendela Wolters), but also need to acknowledge and thank Isak Rydlund (contract expert, LL.M) and Sven Wilson (editor) for believing in our project and giving us latitude to explore creative possibilities on a shoestring budget. Not everyone has met everyone physically – some have only met virtually! – but the mutual trust and respect within this group has truly been amazing!

We hope that after reading our book and having a peek into how we work together, you are inspired to have a go and embark on a project that you've always wanted to do, and collaborate with others to transform possibilities into reality. Anything is possible!

We look forward to reading what has inspired you. To continue the conversation, or if you have any comments and feedback/feedforward please send them to: info@muchadoaboutcoaching.com

Contributors

Yvonne Thackray (MEng, APECS) is a practicing coach, researcher, author (book and papers), blogger and anthropologist. She is a Professional Executive & Personal (PEP) Coach, accredited by APECS, and former Company Secretary and Founding member of the ICF Hong Kong Chapter. She works with clients who are seeking to develop further motivation and presence in leading roles in their projects and organisation. She also works as a researcher in the anthropology of coaching, and sits on a number of working groups of professional body/institutions developing practitioner knowledge and reviewing peer papers.

For more information, please go to *http://the-goodcoach.com/ yvonnethackray-coach/* and *uk.linkedin.com/in/yvonnethackray* **Email:** yvonne@the-goodcoach.com

Charlotte Rydlund (MBA) is an executive and change management coach, author and entrepreneur, trained at Columbia University. She works with leaders, teams and business owners who are experiencing change in their lives and at work. She has managed her own career transition from international Fortune 500 to business owner, and is passionate about supporting others in managing change. She is a business leader, combining her background in marketing and brand management, strategic sourcing and global non-profit work with coaching and training to empower others to succeed.

For more information, please go to *http://the-goodcoach.com/ charlotte-rydlund/* and *ca.linkedin.com/in/charlotterydlund* **Email:** charlotte@the-goodcoach.com

Nicholas Wai (MBA) is an independent executive coach and facilitator based in Hong Kong. With more than 10 years of international corporate experience and a master qualification in coaching from the University of Sydney, he works with multinational and local organizations as well as small business owners and individuals in enhancing personal and professional effectiveness and work-life integration among other areas. Nicholas is also active in promoting coaching in the community, as the company secretary and event organizer of the International Coach Federation Hong Kong Chapter, as well as an active member and event organizer of the Hong Kong Coaching Outreach.

For more information, please go to *http://the-goodcoach.com/ nicholaswai-coach/* or *http://www.linkedin.com/in/nickwai*
Email: nick@the-goodcoach.com

Naomi Dishington (MEd) is an experienced educator and coach, currently working as a career advisor to a diverse group of MBA students. She is passionate about facilitating growth and change with young professionals. Her warm and approachable coaching style draws from the co-active model, and includes asking insightful questions, leading rich conversations, and offering encouraging support.
Email: Naomidish@gmail.com

Wendela Wolters (MSc, RN) is an organizational psychologist, mediator and coach. She assists clients (individuals & companies) in developing effective stress prevention procedures by implementing both work-directed and person-directed interventions. As registered mediator she utilizes her skills in conflict management and mediations, always with a keen eye on creating a win-win situation. She uses an appreciative approach, focused on what works well instead of what doesn't work.

For more details, check out her profile on *http://the-goodcoach. com/wendela-wolters* and *nl.linkedin.com/in/wendela-ho-kang- you*
Email: wendelawolters@gmail.com

Isak Rydlund (LL.M) is a contracting and negotiations expert with a passion for supporting Coaches and developing the field of contracting within the industry. He leverages his knowledge and experience from developing and negotiating multilevel and multi-regional contracts for companies ranging from Sole Proprietorships to Fortune 500. He uses his background in law, business development and strategic negotiations to provide Coaches with understandable and flexible tailored contracts together with training and guidance that the Coach can use with their clients. His approach is to ensure a win-win and ethical outcome for all stakeholders. Isak has been instrumental in the contractual formation of the group, including a tailored international partnership agreement as well as a multi-regional licensing agreement.

For more information see *www.thegybegroup.com* and contact him at *isak@thegybegroup.com* for a free consultation on how he can help you.

Notes on the contractual agreement

The Dilemma:
How should contributing authors be fairly rewarded?

Members involved:
Project Owners, Authors and Contract Expert, LL.M

Background: It's common practice in the coaching industry to freely share and give away one's work and gratefully accept that the recognition from being published in a book is the reward. The agreements which author(s) sign with the owner(s) of the project, will often sign away their rights to the 'essay(s)' and future rewards (if offered) because that is 'the way it works'. The question for us became, "Is this really the only way? Is it not possible to find a better solution in which all the parties involved would and benefit both reputationally and profitably from engaging in the project?"

Our Approach: We engaged a contract expert with an LL.M to write an agreement that reflected our values and offered an alternative legal framework which ensured, as best as possible, that all parties involved in the project would benefit (reputationally and profitably) from this endeavour.

Having a legal agreement is necessary because it protects all parties from possible legal contentions (e.g. intellectual property, ownership, compensation, third-party rights etc.) that may arise after the book is published, and we highly recommend this be a part of your normal practice for any products that are released into a market where profits can be earnt.

We achieved our goal through two clauses, specifically 'licence' and 'compensation'.

- **Licence:** It was important to the group that the authors retained ownership of their own material whilst allowing the project owners to publish their work under the owner's project in perpetuity.

  'The Author shall retain sole and exclusive ownership of all rights, title and interest in and to the Intellectual Property and/or the Works, subject to the licenses granted to Assignee under this Agreement.'

- **Compensation:** With any project there are risks, and by taking those risks one hopes to realise rewards. Through sales of the book we hope not only that each author's reputation is increased, but that we will be able to fairly share some of the financial equity. We used the following approach: a royalty payout as a percentage of net profit on all sales after recouping the cost of goods sold over an agreed period of time. This was agreed by the project owners, and will vary per project. We pledge to use this approach for projects in the future, ensuring fair compensation for every stakeholder's contributions.

  'The Assignee and Author agree to the following complete compensation (Royalty) for the license in order to create a precedent for the industry.'

The result: all the contributing authors signed the agreement and were pleasantly surprised that a possible future financial reward was part of the agreement – a sign of mutual respect between the authors and the project owners. They also remarked that it was a refreshing change and it was something that could be used in future negotiations for similar work.

Contract expert's commentary

Isak Rydlund, LL.M

I*t is very common in the coaching industry to use commercial contracts and service-level agreements (i.e. the coaching contract) that are not written or reviewed by a contract expert, such un-reviewed contracts can lead to a bad experience or even legal liability for the coach. Using contracts that may be unclear, not fully understood by all parties, or that favour the interests of one of the parties (not fair and equitable) may lead to contracts that are unenforceable in a court of law or open the coach up to other risks.*

Understanding the wording, meaning and intent of any contract is key to a positive and transparent working relationship between contracting parties.

In constructing the partnership and the licensing agreements for the RYDWAIRAY™ group, it was imperative to ensure not only the buy-in from all stakeholders, but also a complete understanding of the possibilities and limitations of the agreements. The stakeholders' desire to create a precedent for the industry meant the multi-regional, multi-stakeholder agreements would need to be flexible and easily understood for the coaches and authors while at the same time ensuring a suitable level of legal protection for the partnership and the individuals involved. These criteria were addressed by conducting multiple sessions of expectation-setting, feedback and discussion with the parties to the agreements, both in a group setting and on an individual basis.

Ensuring full transparency and understanding of the roles, responsibilities, ownership and compensation ensures a good base for a long term cooperation, creates a win-win situation for all parties involved, and sets a precedent for the industry that will have long-lasting effects.

Bibliography & references

Albrecht, K. (1979). *Stress and the Manager*. Touchstone.

Barnett, B. (1995). 'Developing Reflection and Expertise: Can Mentors Make the Difference?' *Journal Of Educational Administration*, 33(45).

Biswas-Diener, R. (2012). *The Courage Quotient*. Jossey Bass.

Blanchard, K., Carlos, J.P. & Randolph, A. (2001). *Empowerment Takes More Than a Minute*. Berrett-Koehler.

Bresser, F. (2013). *Coaching across the Globe*. Publish on Demand.

Brock, V. (2008). 'Grounded theory of the roots and emergence of coaching'. *Unpublished D.Phil dissertation*. Maui, HI: International University of Professional Studies

Burt, N.F. (1996). 'The Relationship between Myers-Briggs Type and Individual Preference for Dealing with Organizational Change'. *Published Ph.D dissertation*. Georgia State University, GA, USA.

Cain, S. (2012). *Quiet, The Power of Introverts*. Penguin.

Dagley, G. & AHRI. (2013). *Executive Presence: Influence beyond Authority*.

Dweck, C. (2006). *Mindset*. Ballantine.

Francis, D. (1995). 'The Reflective Journal: A Window to Preservice Teachers' Practical Knowledge'. *Teaching and Teacher Education*, 11(3), 229-241.

Fulghum, R. (1990). *All I really need to know I learned in Kindergarten*. Harper Collins.

Gallway, T. (2008). *The Inner Game of Tennis*. Random House.

Gilbert, W., & Trudel, P. (2001). 'Learning to coach through experience: Reflection in model youth sport coaches'. *Journal of Teaching in Physical Education,* 21, 16-34.

Gold, E.J. (1986). *Life in the Labyrinth.* Gateways Books & Tapes.

Grant, A.M. and Cavanagh, M. (2004). 'Toward a profession of coaching: Sixty-five years of progress and challenges for the future'. *International Journal of Evidence Based Coaching and Mentoring,* 2(1), 7-21.

Grant, A. M. (2005). 'What is evidence-based executive, workplace and life coaching?' *Evidence-based coaching* (1), 1-12.

Grant, A. M. (2006). 'A personal perspective on professional coaching and the development of coaching psychology'. *International Coaching Psychology Review* 1(1), 12-22.

Herzfeld, M. (1985). *The Poetics of Manhood: Contest and Identity in a Cretan Mountain Village.* Princeton University Press.

Kahneman, D. (2011). *Thinking Fast and Slow.* Penguin.

Kimsey-House, H., Kimsey-House, K. and Sandahl, P. (2011). *Co-Active Coaching: Changing Business Transforming Lives.* Nicholas Brealey Publishing.

Larson, M.S. (2013). *The Rise of Professionalism.* Transaction Publishers. Lehrer, J. (2009). *The Decisive Moment: How the Brain Makes Up Its Mind.* Canongate Books Ltd.

Lehrer, J. (2009). *The Decisive Moment: How the Brain Makes Up Its Mind.* Canongate Books Ltd.

Milne, A., Off. B & Shepard, E. (2003). *The Tao of Pooh.* Egmont.

Nouwen, H., McNeill, D., Morrison, D. & Filartiga, J. (2000). *Compassion: A Reflection on the Christian Life.* Bantam Doubleday Dell Publishing Group.

Overbo, J. (2010). 'Using Myers-Briggs Personality Type to Create Culture Adapted to the New Century'. *T+D Magazine,* 64.

Pearman, R. and Albritton, S. (2010) *I'm not Crazy, I'm Just Not You.* Second Edition. Nicholas Brealey Publishing.

Peltier, B. (2009). *The Psychology of Executive Coaching: Theory & Application.* Routledge.

Ridler & Co. (2013). *Ridler Report 2013: Trends in the Use of Executive Coaching.*

Rosen, C. (2008). 'The Myth of Multitasking'. *The New Atlantis,* 20, 105-110.

Salzberg, S. (2011). *Real Happiness: The Power of Meditation.* Workman Pub Co.

Sennet, R. (2003). *Respect: The Formation of Character in an Age of Inequality.* Penguin.

Siegel, D. (2011). *Mindsight: The New Science of Personal Transformation.* Bantam.

Spence, G. (2007). 'GAS Powered Coaching Goal Attainment Scaling and its use in coaching research and practice'. *International Coaching Psychology Review,* 2(2), 155-167.

Stahl, B. & Goldstein, E. (2010). *A Mindfulness-Based Stress Reduction Workbook.* New Harbinger Publications.

Stober, D. R. & Grant, A. M. (2006). *Evidence Based Coaching Handbook: Putting Best Practices to Work for Your Clients.* Wiley.

Whitmore, J. (1992). *Coaching for Performance: GROWing Human Potential and Purpose.* Nicholas Brealey Publishing.

Williams, P. (20 Jan 2004). Coaching and Mentoring International Annual Seminar.

Zander, R. S. & R. (2002). *The Art of Possibility: Transforming Professional and Personal Life.* Penguin.

Online references

Andrea St. George Blog
www.andreastgeorge.blogspot.com

Association for Professional Executive Coaching and Supervision (APECS)
www.apecs.org

How not to spend your whole day on facebook | BigThink.com
http://bigthink.com/think-tank/how-not-to-spend-your-whole-day-on-facebook

3 Areas You Need to Focus on To Get 'Executive Presence... | Business Insider
http://businessinsider.com/3-areas-you-need-tofocus-on-to-get-executive-presence-2013-2

Share Economy: Band-aid solution or promoting... | CBC
http://www.cbc.ca/thecurrent/episode/2014/03/03/share-economy-band-aid-solution-to-real-economic-problems-or-promoting-sustainability/

International Coach Federation
http://coachfederation.org/

Changing families: The post-nuclear age | Economist.com
http://www.economist.com/news/britain/21573548-forget-traditional-family-there-are-now-three-distinct-models-associated

The Enneagram Spectrum of Personality Styles | Jerome Wagner, Ph.D
http://www.enneagramspectrum.com/

Stress Facts | Global Organization for Stress
www.gostress.com

Charles Duhigg On The Power of Habit in Biz and Life... | Goodlifeproject. com
http://www.goodlifeproject.com/charles-duhigg-nyt-reporter-author

Top five regrets of the dying | theguardian.com
http://www.guardian.co.uk/lifeandstyle/2012/feb/01/top-five-regrets-of-the-dying

*Bruce Davis, Ph.D.: There are 50,000 Thoughts Standing... |
Huffingtonpost.com*
http://www.huffingtonpost.com/bruce-davis-phd/healthy-
relationships_b_3307916.html

Facts about Stress | International Stress Management
www.isma.org.uk

*Swisscom chief executive Carsten Schloter who committed... |
Independent.co.uk*
http://www.independent.co.uk/news/world/europe/swisscom-chief-
executive-carsten-schloter-who-committed-suicide-could-not-stop-
looking-at-his-smartphone-8730740.html

*Forget about Setting Goals. Focus on this Instead |
Jamesclear.com*
http://jamesclear.com/goals-systems

How much of communication is really nonverbal? | Nonverbalgroup.com
http://www.nonverbalgroup.com/2011/08/how-much-of-communication-
is-really-nonverbal/

Lucy Jo Palladino, Ph.D website
http://www.lucyjopalladino.com

The Social Learning Theory of Julian B. Rotter
http://psych.fullerton.edu/jmearns/rotter.htm

*Ken Robinson: How to escape education's Death Valley |
Ted.com*
http://www.ted.com/talks/ken_robinson_how_to_escape_education_s_
death_valley.html

Transtheoretical model | Wikipedia, the free encyclopedia
http://en.wikipedia.org/wiki/Transtheoretical_model

*Tuckman's stages of group development | Wikipedia, the free
encyclopedia*
http://en.wikipedia.org/wiki/Tuckman's_stages_of_group_development

Benjamin Zander: The transformative power of classical music | Ted.com
http://www.ted.com/talks/benjamin_zander_on_music_and_passion.
html

*Benjamin Zander's Interpretations of Music: Lessons for Life | YouTube.
com*
https://www.youtube.com/watch?v=J9ZGutYV45Q

Bringing science into the art of coaching | ZengerFolkman.com
http://www.zengerfolkman.com/media/articles/ZFA-Science-Art-of-
Coaching.pdf

For quotes: *BrainyQuote.com* (Anaïs Nin, Aristotle, Eleanor Roosevelt)

www.ingramcontent.com/pod-product-compliance
Lightning Source LLC
Chambersburg PA
CBHW071147200326
41519CB00018B/5143